This is a well written book on the role of the church in society. The brilliant dialogue running through each chapter gives it depth and conceptual flavor. Based on thorough scholarship, its suggestions can only improve the church-state relationship. It is a must read for leaders within the church and society.

- Pastor Ken Wilson
Holding Forth Christian Centre
Milton Keynes

The Mandates of the Church

With compliments from

Rich Ayo Adekoya

AuthorHouse™ UK
1663 Liberty Drive
Bloomington, IN 47403 USA
www.authorhouse.co.uk
Phone: 0800.197.4150

Unless otherwise stated scripture quotations are taken from the Holy Bible, New International Version®. NIV® Copyright© 1973, 1978, 1984 by International Bible Society. Used by permission of Zondervan. All rights reserved.

Scripture quotations marked NIV are taken from the Holy Bible, New International Version®. NIV® Copyright© 1973, 1978, 1984 by International Bible Society. Used by permission of Zondervan. All rights reserved.

Scripture quotations are taken from the King James Version (KJV) of the Bible—Public Domain.

Scripture quotations taken from the New English Bible, copyright© Cambridge University Press and Oxford University Press 1961, 1970. All rights reserved.

Scripture quotations marked NKJV are taken from the New King James Version. Copyright© 1982 by Thomas Nelson, Inc. Used by permission. All rights reserved.

© 2015 Rich Ayo Adekoya. All rights reserved.

No part of this book may be reproduced, stored in a retrieval system, or transmitted by any means without the written permission of the author.

Published by AuthorHouse 06/29/2015

ISBN: 978-1-5049-4473-1 (sc)
ISBN: 978-1-5049-4474-8 (e)

Print information available on the last page.

Any people depicted in stock imagery provided by Thinkstock are models, and such images are being used for illustrative purposes only. Certain stock imagery © Thinkstock.

This book is printed on acid-free paper.

Because of the dynamic nature of the Internet, any web addresses or links contained in this book may have changed since publication and may no longer be valid. The views expressed in this work are solely those of the author and do not necessarily reflect the views of the publisher, and the publisher hereby disclaims any responsibility for them.

To my Saviour and Redeemer, Jesus Christ

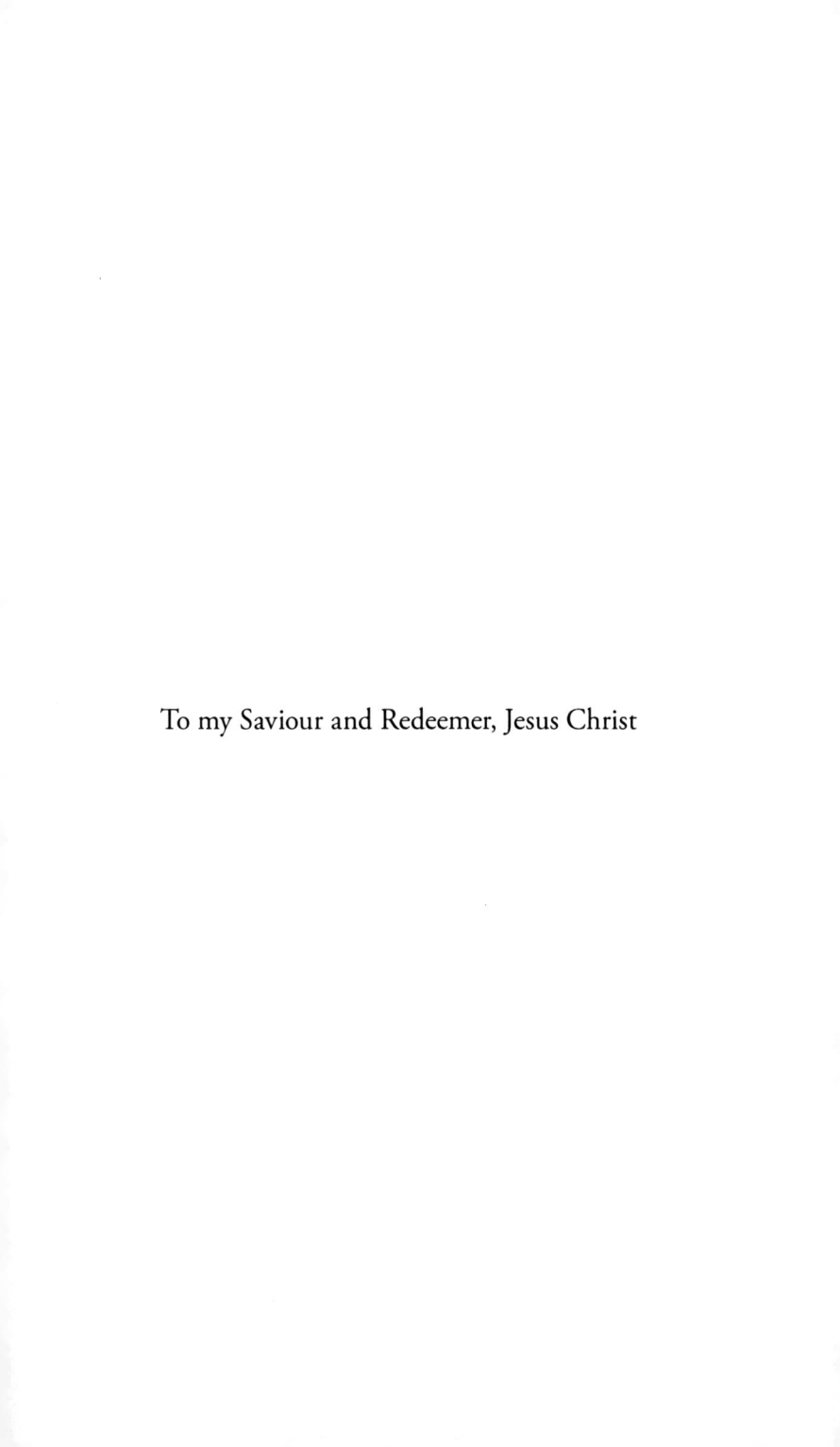

Foreword

The pages that follow tackle a key issue that currently faces the church around the world, namely, whether and how to be involved in the vast number of social and political problems that ordinary people around the world face in their day to day lives. The failure to produce realistic solutions results in the daily misery of poverty, oppression of various kinds, disease, violence and crime experienced by millions. Perhaps the worst kind of poverty is the poverty of hope that causes the kind of acute despair leading to ten of thousands choosing to risk their lives in extreme conditions in order to escape the grinding despair of their lived experience.

It seems impossible to argue that Christians have nothing to say about these conditions or that the church as a social institution has no contribution to make to improving the lives of millions. Yet, that is precisely what some do argue. They make the case that Christianity has more to do with the issue of heaven than earth, that individual Christians should live highly moral lives and that the effect of this right living will eventually improve the world, that the mandate of the church is not social but evangelistic and that there is no evidence that Jesus came to change society but to make individual disciples.

What can we say about such an argument? It is certainly true that Jesus did not found a political party, or organize a social welfare programme. He was a rabbi, a teacher and although he demonstrated great compassion towards individuals he seemed to be primarily concerned about the spiritual condition of those he met and not so much about their social situation. Yet, weighed against these considerations is the passion that Jesus displayed for the coming of the Kingdom of God. That agenda had a context and a meaning in the history and prophetic tradition of the people of Israel. In other words the Old Testament gives a particular content to the meaning of the Kingdom that Jesus came to proclaim.

It is clear that the early church showed a compassionate response to the sufferings of those they met. They developed a reputation as a people that showed love to those around them. That love was often demonstrated as caring for widows and orphans, for developing prison ministry, becoming involved in establishing schools and hospitals, working to prevent infanticide in short by siding with the weak and helpless.

Of course that does not amount to a political and social programme but as the church became more influential in society, it was hard to avoid the consequences of being a social institution to which people turned for spiritual and social guidance. The issue of how we live together, of practical ethics, of the common good and of opposition to evil became more and more urgent as the witness of the church became more and more successful.

The question of political and social involvement has never been a controversial subject for the Roman Catholic tradition but it has been a considerable concern for the Pentecostal, Evangelical, and Charismatic tradition

The Mandates of the Church

that has become so powerfully present in much of the developing world over the previous half century.

There are particular reasons why this issue has been troublesome for this particular tradition. The question has its origins in the particular development of evangelicalism in the early 20th century in Europe and North America. The activity of missions emanating from this tradition succeeding in exporting the controversy to almost every part of the world. It has been presented as a clear option between social action or evangelism. The claim of evangelicals in the early part of the 20th century was that the church only has a mandate to preach the gospel (evangelize) and not to meddle in social and political action. Individuals might do what they could by living good lives to influence society but the church as an institution should steer well clear of such an entanglement.

This conclusion might seem extraordinary given the role of evangelicals in the changing of society for the good in the 19th century but there are particular historical and ecclesial reasons for this peculiar development. The healing of the divide between evangelism and social concern was first signaled by the Lausanne movement in 1974 and it has often been Christians from the developing continents of Africa, South America, and Asia that have led the way.

Richard Adekoya's excellent work, tackles this set of issues in a very thorough way. By looking at the issues through the lens of the Bible, church history and sociological analysis he makes a powerful theological case for the involvement of the church in the societies in which it finds itself called to give a witness.

Understandably and helpfully there is a particular emphasis on Nigeria, a nation which he knows well. By choosing Nigeria as a kind of case history the broader, general case is given a particular and penetrating illustration that strengthens his wider argument.

There is of course a difference between social action and social engagement. We might still object as Christians to the kind of social action that seeks to champion a cause or an outcome that often brings conflict by virtue of the aggressive means that the campaigners adopt. The social engagement of the church is more conciliatory, more nuanced, seeking peace and justice for all alongside the implementation of reform. That kind of engagement is what Richard argues for. I am happy that he has produced this work and commend it to potential readers as a thorough treatment of an important subject.

Dr. Martin Robinson
Principal and Chief Executive
Springdale College: Together in Mission
Rowheath Pavilion
Heath Road
Bournville
Birmingham
B30 1HH

Preface

This book is an offshoot of a doctoral thesis, and it has taken approximately two years in its preparation. For the author, it has been a quite rewarding exercise in patience, perseverance, and persistence. The journey began when I was a doctoral student at Mattersey Hall College in the United Kingdom. I was puzzled about the state of the Nigeria nation, when my colleagues asked rhetorically questions like 'What can the church do to help?' or 'What role has the church played so far?' or 'What ought to be the role of the church in the society?' These and many more were among the thought-provoking questions that featured at the DMIN seminar series at Mattersey.

In response, this book addresses those questions and many others, focusing on the issues of politics, social change, the church, social development, society, and the theological response to socio-political engagement. Drawing on practical study and observations, it offers biblical insight into the legitimacy of the church's involvement in the socio-political order of society and how its social and political actions are means of fulfilling its mission.

This book brings to the fore the intertwined relationship between the church and society on one hand

and the relationship between the church and the state on the other hand. It also highlights how this relationship could collaboratively lead to positive developments for the citizens and society in general.

This book is a product of empirical and practical study of Nigerian churches via their practices, dogmas, and local contexts. It involves first-hand observation of the everyday lives of the people within those contexts, along with their organisation, modes of operation, and the effects of their activities on the socio-political development in the state. The Christian church has become a formidable force in Nigeria today; however, social ills exist unabated. Lagos State is the spiritual headquarters of many church denominations in Nigeria. It is the commercial capital of the nation, and all other states of the federation are well represented there to the point where it is often referred to as 'mini Nigeria'. Because Lagos is so representative in nature, the study has focused on Lagos. The presence of churches in Lagos State is overwhelming.

The hope is that this book will contribute to the body of literature already in circulation about the role of the church in society and how the symbiotic relationship can be improved.

Rich Ayo Adekoya
London, United Kingdom
April 13, 2015

Acknowledgement

The challenge of rewriting my doctoral thesis into a book or two was a scented exercise and I am particularly grateful to God for the grace, strength, good health and guidance at every stage. His faithfulness over the years has been awesome; to Him alone I ascribe all honour, glory and praise for accomplishing this task. The huge support I got in the course of writing this book is overwhelming, as many creative individuals offered me assistance and advice. These 'heroes' of mine have all contributed one way or another to the preparation and completion of this book.

I wish to personally thank the following people for their contributions to my inspiration and knowledge and other helps in creating this book: Professor Afe Adogame, Dr. Anne Dyer, Dr. Babatunde Adedibu and Dr. Gideon Bakare, they challenged my thinking and helped to give this book a shape. Dr. Martin Robinson deserves my gratitude for his mentorship role in my academic pursuit and writing of the foreword for this book.

I am equally grateful to my pastors and spiritual fathers, Pastor Gabriel Ajeigbe and Bishop James O. Odedeji. They are sources of inspiration to me on what the Church should be and their involvement and that of Pastor Gibson Ezimah at different stages of this book helped immensely to improve this document.

I need to also mention Mummy F. O. Osofisan and Gbenga Osofisan for their assistance during my research in Lagos, their efforts helped make my tasks less stressful. It would be unfair not to mention Ken Wilson and Jay Oguntuase, they kept me on track with scholastic discussions most times. Thank you all for investing your time to support me.

Finally, I would never have embarked on this journey without my wife Bukola (Mimi) and this is no exaggeration. She has been so supportive and understanding; she stood by me every step of the way, thank you dear. To the Rich-Mimi team, Debbie, Sharon, Precious and Israel (my beloved children), thanks for giving Daddy the time off to put these thoughts together, God bless you all.

Contents

Title Page iii
Dedication v
Foreword vii
Preface xi
Acknowledgement xiii
Contents xv
Epigraph Credits xvii
Introduction xix

Chapter One
The Church–State Controversy 1

Chapter Two
Understanding Missiology 8

Chapter Three
Philosophic Considerations of Church and State 20

Chapter Four
Biblical Reflections on Church and
Social Involvement 41

Chapter Five
The 'How' of the Church's Engagement in Society.....54

Chapter Six
The Contribution of the Church to Lagos Society 76

Bibliography.. 101
About the Author 121

Epigraph Credits

I want to thank all well-meaning individuals, organisations and trust that permitted me to use their quotations as epigraphs in this book;

Dallas Willard, The Spirit of the Disciplines: Understanding How God Changes Lives (Harper San Francisco, 1991)

Ronald Reagan and The Ronald Reagan Library

Oscar A. Romero, The Violence of Love (Orbis Books, 2004)

Mother Teresa and The Mother Teresa Center

John Ortberg, The Me I Want to Be: Becoming God's Best Version of You (Zondervan, 2014)

Introduction

It is a plain truth that the church and the state must collide at some point or another. Can the church serve society better than the politicians?

There are divergent opinions today about the roles the church should be playing in the society given the new global culture and the rapid shifts in education, technology, industry, and economics. Despite the presence of the church in our communities, the inhumanity of man against man is on the increase. Individuals and families often feel powerless and voiceless.

Social evils such as corruption, injustice, violence, racial discrimination, and drug addiction have permeated every level of society in an unprecedented manner. If this decadence lingers on unchecked, it will eventually erode moral values and any sense of justice and community spirit in society. It therefore becomes imperative for the church to take a stand either to ignore the prevailing societal problems and continue its spiritual assignments, believing that it has no control over the systems and circumstances, or alternatively to see itself as a watchman in society that needs to make a difference in the world by getting involved and committed to the social-political changes necessary in whichever community it finds itself.

These issues need to be confronted. The causes of all these societal evils need to be known and dealt with. The symptoms must be eradicated wherever possible, and endemic evils in state policies and structures also need to be checked. Until this is done, the prevailing circumstances will clog the wheel of progress and stability in society.

There are those who would want the church to keep out of politics and concentrate on citizens' spiritual life. However, they believe it can be socially involved in society by providing certain social welfare to the populace, just not social action. They claim that the structures of contemporary society are progressively becoming more antagonistic and hostile to the church's worldview; therefore it should only be concerned with the spiritual and social well-being of those within its immediate constituency. However, the question is, can you be involved socially and not involved politically?

On the other hand there are those who believe that the church's mission is to transform society and that the point of division between church and the state is sometimes very difficult to identify. The church as People of God (that is, Christians) is called to influence the course of events in the world and to create a just society where social justice and peace reign in every area of human life. Through exemplary lifestyles and selfless services, the church is expected to demonstrate how to live as a community of people free from prejudice, hatred, pride, avarice, while exercising leadership as servanthood.

By and large, the school of thought that advocates that the church should abstain from the socio-political world also condemns most of what is happening around the world as sin, and the more the church attempts to act as an agent of change in any given society, the more there will be opposition who are always ready to promote reasons why its social and political involvement in society could do more harm than good.

The questions are:

- What is the position of the Bible on the roles the church should play in the state?
- What is the nature of the church?
- Should the church's social responsibilities be limited to charitable activities alone?
- Must the church be politically detached from the state?
- How best can the church help to bring about meaningful changes to the state?
- Thus far, has the church succeeded in the task of being an agent of social and political changes in any society?

Chapter One

The Church–State Controversy

The world can no longer be left to mere diplomats, politicians, and business leaders. They have done the best they could, no doubt. But this is an age for spiritual heroes—a time for men and women to be heroic in their faith and in spiritual character and power.

— Dallas Willard, *The Spirit of the Disciplines: Understanding How God Changes Lives*

There has been an endless chain of questions about how the church should work alongside the state. The separation of church and state has from time immemorial been of global concern, at least in countries where churches do exist in high statistical proportion to the population. The separation of the church from the state, as used here, refers to the detachment as much as possible in the relationship between organized religion and the state's political apparatus, so that the integrity of each of the institutions is preserved (Eberle 2011: 3). The separation of the church from the state is a two-edged sword that can be both constructive and destructive. Darien Auburn McWhirter explained that it is not just about curtailing government's actions towards the church and other religions, but also curbing the church (or any other religious body) from meddling in affairs of state. Neither the church nor any other religious group can compel or force the government to do anything (McWhirter 1994: 124).

Although the legitimate boundaries that define the spheres of influence of the two might be different, they might be two established institutions independent of each other but having overlapping functions. Their activities are often expressed through their members. Some of the populace belong to the church, yet they are also active members of political parties, expressing their moral and social ideas in the political order. Erwin Fahlbusch, a professor in the Department of Systematic Theology, Faculty of Protestant Theology at the University of Frankfurt, could not agree less. He states that 'state and church often include same people, but they represent different aims and styles of work.' This is an issue in which history, politics, and theology play vital roles (Fahlbusch 2008: 188).

Charles Taliaferro and J. Paul Griffiths, both professors of Philosophy whose specialization is Theology and the Philosophy of Religion, state that the church by its nature is a combination of Christian social responsibilities to society and the spiritual well-being of people within its constituency (Taliaferro and Griffiths 2003: 459). Meanwhile, the state's mandate also has a lot to do with social responsibilities to the same society. These dual associations and common missions to the same society create complications and controversies. Both sides of the discussion seem to have valid arguments that need deeper and careful examination in order for us to be unbiased in striking a balance.

Moreover, in a pluralistic society there will always be a diversity of respectable yet conflicting outlooks (Wagner 1999: 531), and sometimes one must combine them to get a reasonable result. This is what Bishop Bokeleale, the former President of the Church of Christ in Congo, refers to as 'collaboration' (*ThirdWay* 1979: 21). Saïd Amir Arjomand, a professor of Sociology at the state University of New York, described it thus:

> The church protect society from the state repression and demand from the state protection of individual human and civil rights, but it stopped short of demanding institutionalization of full political rights. The state, in turn, needed the church mediation in order to obtain from the society at least passive compliance. (1993: 137)

In Western society today, a lot has been written about the separation of church and state, and the influence of the church is waning on a daily basis. The approach varies in different countries. For example, in France and Turkey, the Laicite's principle is adopted (Boer 2007: 13). The United Kingdom took a socially secularised stance by maintaining a constitutionally recognised state religion, and yet other churches and faiths co-exist (Bretherton 2011: 36). The German constitution pledges freedom of religion, though there are still officially recognised churches (Bezanson 2010: 185). Norway recently specifically abolished having any state-organised religion while involving the populace in paying taxes for the provision of church ministers' maintenance (Fraser). In the United State of America, it remains an on-going contentious topic and an issue of impassioned debate (Boris and Steuerle [eds.] 2006: 23). The founding fathers insisted that there should be no state control of any religion and that no religion (for the original colonists, Christianity and its dissenting forms) should influence state-controlled institutions such as schools (Nanda,2006: 119). Geographically and historically, there have been great swings and changes in the issue of the separation of church and state. Despite these variations, the effect ultimately is the same: the gap between the church and the state is widening and 'collaboration' between the two is being cut back.

Although, many factors have been suggested for the waning influence of the church's influence in the public square, apart from the separation of church and state, there has also been a shift in culture in contemporary Western society, whereby the personal faith of Christians has remained private. An American evangelical author, Nancy Pearcey, claims that it is a divine mandate for man to develop culture; therefore, if the culture is changing and modernity or secularity is invading what used to be the Christians' space, Christians ought to rise to the challenge by engaging with society expressly and should not live out their faith privately and remain unfulfilled (Pearcey 2008: 68–69). Missiologist Leslie Newbigin (1986: 44) and church growth experts Eddie Gibbs and R. K. Bolger (Bolger 2006: 17) agree strongly with Pearcey.

Christian Smith, the author of *Christian America, What Evangelicals Really Want* challenged Christians to make a show of their faith in the public as the 'salt' and the 'light' to the rest of society (2002: 157–158). The Christian faith, though personal, should not be seen or practised as 'legally permissible private eccentricity' that cannot be exhibited publicly (*The Observatory* 2010). According to Newbigin, 'the church is nothing other than movement launched into the life of the world' (Newbigin 1989: 221)

By contrast, governments in many African countries are seeking ways to partner with the church and with other religious bodies to better society, realising that they are integral to civil society. There are divergent opinions today in Africa, and in Nigeria in particular, in regard to the roles the church should be playing in society. Many have argued that the narrative contents of the Bible are solid bases for the church's social responsibility and societal involvement. Moreover, despite the presence of the church in our communities, the inhumanity of man against man is on the increase, and people feel powerless in the face of the challenges facing our society (Adewuji 2007: 97). Some members of the church are either directly or indirectly affected by these societal ills. However, are these enough reasons for the church to take up the responsibility acting as social crusader?

The corruption and injustice that have infiltrated every level of society, especially in Africa, is unprecedented. Peter W. Vakunta, an African scholar, lecturing at the Department of French and Italian at the University of Wisconsin, Madison, reckons that it has become impossible to ignore these cankers that are eating deep into the marrow of Africa's social structure (Vakunta 2008: 7) and are tolerated by people at all levels (Meur 2008: 145). You either 'win by hook or crook' (The Bombay Saint Paul Society 2007: 88) or your freedom remains a dream. The norm is 'if you cannot beat them, you join them' (Dawkins 2006: 33). The citizens of various nations and communities are on a daily basis witnessing growing rates of violent crimes, sexual promiscuity, drug abuse, and general lawlessness resulting from bad governance, poor leadership, and a host of other factors (UN Habitat 2005: 5–37).

These factors need to be confronted. The causes of all these societal evils need to be identified and dealt with. The symptoms must be eradicated where possible, and endemic evils in states' policies and structures also need to be checked. According to Leslie Paul Thiele, a political theorist at the University of Florida, 'progress and growth are products of the struggle between two opposing forces' (1992: 81) Therefore, there is a need for stakeholders within the polity to take action.

The church is one of the stakeholders in any society where churches exist and remain in high statistical proportion to the population. Hence, it is dangerous not just for society but also for the church itself to remain aloof in a situation that not only affects its members and its eventual penetration of the society with the gospel message.

The story of Nigeria is a good example, and it is the focal point here. The Nigerian constitution of 1999 stipulates that Nigeria is a secular state where freedom of religion and worship is guaranteed (Sharma 2009: 41). Historically, the church has been actively involved in the development of the nation. According to Apkenpuun Dzurgba of the University of Ibadan, the pre-independence church in Nigeria was not just a major intellectual inspiration to Nigerian activists who later emerged as national leaders, but it also laid the foundations for the socio-economic development of modern Nigeria (1991).

The church, as an integral part of civil society, had collaborated with the government in several ways, and it had opposed the same when the need arose, especially during the military regimes. However, the end of the military junta saw the gradual withdrawal of some Christian leaders and churches, probably because there is now a democratic government in place. This notwithstanding, a few are still in the forefront of the development of democracy, good governance, and making society a better place for all.

The relationship between the socio-political issues, the state, the church, and social development cannot be separated. According to Afe Adogame, a senior lecturer in World Christianity and Religious Studies at the University of Edinburgh, 'all social phenomena within any given group or societies are interrelated' (1999) Hence, when topics like the church and the state are discussed, religion as a social phenomenon cannot be discussed in isolation, but rather as a unit in a recurring interactive relationship with other social units (1999). In light of this, the relationship between the church and the state and the realities of our time raise the following questions:

- How is the church going to get involved and not get caught up in the socio-political web of the secular leaders?
- Is there any solid biblical basis for this involvement?

These issues are worth examining, and that is what this book is all about.

Chapter Two

Understanding Missiology

Our government needs the church, because only those humble enough to admit they're sinners can bring democracy the tolerance it requires to survive.

– *Ronald Reagan*

It will be good to have a background knowledge of what the church is all about—its origin, role, and nature. To better appreciate the subject matter of this piece, there is a need to understand the idea of missiology as it affects the church and society. I will be referring to Andrew Walls, a professor with long experience of West Africa, who stated that 'missiology is theology that takes culture seriously' (1991: 146–155).

This book is ultimately a piece of missiological theology, an aspect of practical theology. The discipline 'missiology' has been variously described by missiologists and theologians. However, to buttress Walls' description

The Mandates of the Church

of missiology, Raymond F. Culpepper emphasizes the importance of culture to a missionary when he says:

> When missionaries go to a foreign culture, they must (i) learn about the culture, (ii) respect the culture, (iii) communicate to the culture, and (iv) reach the lost within the culture with the message of salvation. (2009: 159)

He sees culture as vital aspect of a successful mission enterprise and missiology as a tool to understand the culture and guide mission practitioners in their mission endeavours. He defines missiology as that area of practical theology that investigates the mandate, message, and mission of the Christian church and the nature of missionary work (2009: 159), whereas practical theology has been described as 'a way of doing theology that takes seriously local contexts and practices and the everyday lives of persons in those contexts' (Mercer 2005: 13). It generally relates to every facet of human practices and particularly to how Christian faith is personified in *daily life*. John Pritchard says it 'scrutinizes the everyday life of the church, in the light of the gospel, in a dialogue that both shapes Christian practice and influences the world' (Vanhoozer, Bartholomew, and Treier 2005: 612).

Richard Osmer identifies four key questions and tasks that would normally help in undertaking practical theology (Osmer 2008: 4):

- What is going on? (Descriptive-empirical task)
- Why is this going on? (Interpretative task)
- What ought to be going on? (Normative task)
- How might we respond? (Pragmatic task)

It is aimed at improving the church's life and re-appraises the way Christians live in society. These are necessary questions that this book will have to address in order get to the root of the prevailing situation in Lagos State, Nigeria and the role the church is playing there. Therefore, these questions will be helpful in proffering solutions or suggestions.

Biblically, the church and individual Christians should be interested in everything God created, including politics, governance, society, religion, people, and their living conditions (Romans 13: 1–7). The intentions of God, the purpose of the church, and the tasks of connecting with culture and religion are of paramount importance if a mission is to be practiced appropriately—hence the efforts of the theologians to encourage missiology. John Roxborogh, a Christian biographer and mission historian, succinctly summarises the importance and purpose of missiology when he submits that missiology is theology thinking about the purpose of the church within and outside of itself and about the mission of God. He noted that 'Since Christian mission is directed towards the world, missiology is also concerned with culture and with people of other faiths' (Roxborogh 2013). This is what this study seeks to achieve, thinking theologically about the mission of God and the purpose of the church outside of itself, especially in the context of the culture or the society in which it finds itself. Hence, the church needs to understand itself, its identity, its purpose, and the culture in which it exists.

The changes in the understanding of mission resulted in many faces of mission, whereby mission could no longer be regarded as geographical expansion but rather as the participation of the church in the mission of Triune

God to redeem the whole creation (Bevans and Schroeder 2004: 309). The new theology of mission emerged with views that are emphasising *missio Dei*, God's mission. 'The starting point for mission is that God is a missionary God who is active in the world' (Gibbs and Bolger 2006: 52). However, missiology helps mission practitioners to analyse theoretically and practically reflect on doing Christian mission appropriately (Friedli et al., 2010: 73). Consequently, missiology guides the understanding and practices of the church in its social actions and its roles in the event of cultural and political change in the societies, while still expressing the Christian faith.

Engaging the Debate: Global Perspective

In recent decades, a lot seems to have been written about the mission of the church in and to society. For example, Andrew Kirk, formerly Director of the Centre for Mission and World Christianity at the Selly Oak Colleges and the University of Birmingham, wrote about how the church should be the missionary and the individual Christian a witness. In his book *What Is Mission? Theological Explorations,* Kirk explored the concept of mission and identified seven major missiological themes (culture, evangelism, peace, justice, other religions, partnership, and ecology). He contends that the church's main tasks in the world are:

- stewarding (the church's involvement in keeping and overseeing the material resources of creation)
- service (the church's mission of serving the needs of human beings without discrimination)
- witnessing (the preaching of the truth of the gospel and living out the same)

- justice (the church's involvement in the creation of a just society)
- community (the church's duty to show the way in terms of living together in community)

These five tasks as identified by Kirk collectively and fully articulate the tasks of the church in society and the world in general. Mission affects all of these areas of life, and the theology of mission involves the church in a profound study of each element. Ronald J. Sider submits that 'both evangelism and social transformation offered at this moment in history...' A genuinely biblical perspective inseparably interrelates and intertwines evangelism and social responsibility without equating or confusing the one with the other (1993: 16).

He further argues that evangelism is just an aspect of the mission of the church which primarily deals with inviting non-Christians to embrace the gospel, while social action is the other aspect and its 'primary goal is improving the physical, socio-economic and political well-being of people through relief, development and structural change' (1993: 165). John Stott (2008: 25) and Donald English (Harris 1998) buttressed this view. They believed mission involves evangelism and cultural mandates. The cultural mandate is seen as social action and the struggle for justice. In every aspect of personal and corporate manifestations of Christian faith, there exists an emergent relationship between social action and evangelism as an acknowledged standard of practice.

The distinction between evangelism and social action is very crucial to this discourse, as is the importance of the two to the mission of the church to society. At the International Congress on World Evangelization at

Lausanne in 1974, it was unanimously agreed that the mission of the church is best represented by both cultural and evangelistic mandates (Jonathan Lewis [ed.] 1994) and recently a better expressed purpose of the church emerged at the Lambeth Conference of 1988 in defining 'mission'. It is sometimes stated as the five marks of mission:

(i) to proclaim the good news of the gospel,
(ii) to teach, baptise, and nurture new believers,
(iii) to respond to human needs by loving service,
(iv) to seek to transform unjust structures of society, and
(v) to strive to safeguard the integrity of creation, to sustain and renew the life of the earth (Cray 2004: 156).

A closer look at these five marks will make us think back to the five tasks of the church as identified by Kirk, and all are submerged in the two mandates agreed at ICWE, Lausanne in 1974. While the first two are basically *evangelistic mandate,* the last three are *cultural mandate,* and they are all primarily articulating the difference the church engaged in mission makes to the world. It seems a balanced expression of evangelistic and cultural mandates of the church's mission.

According to Peter C. Wagner, the theologian and missiologist, the *cultural mandate,* which authors like Emmanuel Katongole (2010: 58) and Jonathan Lewis (1994) termed 'Christian social responsibilities', and the *evangelistic mandate* are both essential parts of the biblical mission of the church (Wagner 1994). These two mandates are the focal points of this piece of work.

Matthew Goheen and Craig Bartholomew (Bartholomew 2008: 66), Carl Braaten (1998: 65), Ignatius Swart (2006: 7), and Nancy Pearcey all agree that the church should not only be involved in the welfare level of social transformation but also in the sphere of the politics of ideas, which are its cultural mandate. Pearcey states that cultural mandate is the original purpose of the church. She writes, 'Christians are to redeem entire cultures, not just individuals.' (Pearcey 2004: 17) However, William Hendriksen, a New Testament scholar and writer of Bible commentaries, disagrees with Pearcey and company. He posited that any other mandate outside the evangelistic mandate is a distraction to the church and a hindrance that prevents it fulfilling its mission.

Hendriksen was not alone in this postulation. Arthur W. Pink (1953: 48–49), Martin Lloyd-Jones (1991: 158), and R. T. France (2007: 177) all agreed. In their position, it appears that the cultural mandate is hardly recognised. Meanwhile, there is the biblical account of Acts 2, 6, and 13, where people got converted, social needs arose, and the church rose to the challenge by meeting those needs. It is debatable if the gospel would have made the same impact in the world today if the church and individual Christians were not involved in social services or social actions. Consequently, there is a need to explore the rationale for the Christian churches' interactions with diverse social and political problems in society.

With the cultural mandate, different perceptions arose concerning the role of the church in society conflicting or interfering with the government's activities or policies, and hence, the debate on the separation of church and state arose. Although the debate is fragmentary, the contributions of the church to society cannot be overlooked.

The Mandates of the Church

The relationship between socio-political issues, the state, the church, and social development cannot be separated. However, P. T. Jersid (Jersid 2000: 39), Robert J. Wicks (2000: 548), and Rowan Ireland (1991: 169), have all challenged Christians to think ingeniously and creatively to articulate the vision of an expanded spirituality by participating in the process of the church's mission to transform the society in the light of the values of the kingdom of God.

Despite these positions, some have argued that adoption of the doctrine of separation of church and state has not in any way shut the church out of relevance in society. The church, according to this school of thought, still has major roles to play in the state. According to Xuanmeng Yu, a professor of philosophy from a communist and Christian-minority nation, 'churches and other religious organizations as an important sector of civil society constantly provide the checks and balances to government authorities, which provides a better chance for a healthy development in the society' (1997: 79). Helen Rose Fuchs Ebaugh agreed. The professor and department chair of sociology at the University of Houston strengthened Xuanmeng Yu's submission that the church still has a lot to offer society despite the purported separation of church and state. She argues that religious institutions strongly influence politics;

> Religious institutions fulfil three separate but complementary roles in politics: (1) as incubators for civic skills, (2) as agents for mobilization, and (3) as information providers. Church leaders take stands on political issues, they endorse candidates and

> they allow their churches to be sites where debate and mobilization occurs. (2006: 402)

This is the typical situation in Nigeria. Hence, the issue of religious values and the relationship between church and state cannot be waved aside. Religious faiths and their values support the growth of democracy and the development of society.

Local Nigerian Sources Appraised

The church's mission is religious, but it is not restricted to the teaching and preaching of the gospel. The mission also includes the renewal and improvement of the society where it finds itself. Mission is intrinsic to the church, and to be fittingly so, it has to be missionary within and without. The church promotes national unity and contributes to economic development, inculcating good morals and character in members for the benefits of the larger society. This is the view held by many of the Christian churches in Nigeria. For example, Professor Obiora Ike, an ordained Catholic priest and a scholar and author, when he was answering questions on the legitimacy of the church's participation in political processes and its contribution to the civil society, argued as follows:

> Christian churches have both a mandate and a mission to assist in this search for answers to these questions, based on their organizational, institutional, and technical capacity, as well as their personnel and their many years of local and international experience founded upon credible human and spiritual values. Christian churches have a role to play in transforming the social order. (2013)

The Mandates of the Church

According to him, the Christian churches have the potential to transform and complement the government's effort on many fronts, including inculcating moral values in citizens, at least those within the church constituencies, which helps in promotion of core values and principles that sustain the nation (2013).

Associate Professor P. I. Odozor of the Department of Theology at the University of Notre Dame, agreed with Ike's submission and further asserts that the saving mission of the church has an intrinsic social dimension whereby the church helps to form consciences in political life and stimulate greater insight into the authentic requirements of justice and egalitarian society (2008: 40–58). Professor O. Nnoli (1978: 128) and Ogbu U. Kalu (2013) both agreed. They argued that religion generally shapes and influences human life and thoughts, and when properly harnessed, it forms the basis of good governance.

The church is becoming increasingly aware of the fact that its cultural mandate goes beyond lending helping hands to the poor and the deprived in society. The transformation of social structures and institutions is of equal importance, and this is why it is necessary to evaluate the activities of the church in society.

There will always be connections one way or another between the church and the state in a secular society, even if no faith is established as a state religion. For instance, as recently as 2005, the administration of Olusegun Obasanjo convened a government-sponsored National Political Reform Conference (NPRC) with the objective of reforming the political system and making recommendations on aspects of the nation's constitution that needed to be amended (Aro 2013), and among the delegates to the conference were respected clergymen representing the church and Christian interests.

Most of these ministers and priests had been at the forefront of agitation for democratic rule, a just and egalitarian society bereft of any prejudice. In recognition of the different denominations existing within the church, representation cut across this boundary. One of the clergy was appointed the joint secretary of the conference, Rev. Fr. Matthew Kukah. In May 1999, Father Kukah had been appointed to the Human Rights Violations Investigation Commission (aka Oputa Panel) to probe the human rights abuses of past Nigerian military regimes. In 2005, he was appointed secretary of the National Political Reforms Conference. In 2006, he was again appointed as the presidential facilitator of the Ogoni Peace Process in the Niger Delta. This would not have happened if he and other clergies had confined themselves to the four walls of their churches and held on to just the evangelistic mandate alone.

It should be noted that other faiths were also represented on the NPRC. The secularism of the nation is a political system based on the separation of religion and government, aimed at eliminating discrimination on the basis of religion (Khan 2003: 38). There are over two hundred and fifty ethnic groups in Nigeria, speaking over four thousand languages and dialects (Adelegan 2012: 20). They have diverse cultural and religious backgrounds, so it takes a church that really understands the cultural nuances of this type of set up to contribute meaningfully to a national discourse.

Overall, it is important to build a robust society, develop a people-centred democracy, and offer good governance for the whole country, taking into account the importance of religion and politics to the people in society. From the above arguments, the church and the state are interrelated, and both are necessary for society. They are social phenomena that cannot be divorced from each other. However, it is pertinent to note that the role of the church in the state and vice-versa could be restricted by individual preferences, doctrinal disposition, government policies, and the composition of the society. However, they will keep on influencing each other. This suggests that the church and the state could have a meaningful and successful interactive relationship in a secular state like Nigeria. Society at large stands to benefit from such a relationship if both sides play their roles genuinely.

Chapter Three

Philosophic Considerations of Church and State

One of the penalties of refusing to participate in politics is that you end up being governed by your inferiors.
— Plato

Key Concepts
For a better appreciation of the objectives of this book, it is perhaps a good idea to attempt definitions and descriptions of some key terms. This will help the author delineate boundaries and help the reader relate accurately to the author's perspective so that both can settle on a single understanding of these terms. These terms includes politics, social change, church, development, and society.

Politics
Politics is the management of power in society. It is about the acquisition and the exercise of power. The

authors of the *Oxford Advanced Learner's Dictionary of Current English* succinctly define politics as 'matters concerned with acquiring or exercising power, within a group or an organisation' (Hornby et al., 2005: 893). Another dictionary defines it as 'the activities and affairs involved in managing a state or a government.' These two definitions seem appropriate in describing politics from this book's perspective. However, Maduabuchi F. Dukor's definition will be used as a working definition in this book. He defines the term politics as 'the struggle for power which itself is the authority to determine or formulate and execute decisions and policies which must be accepted by the society' (2003: 26).

Maduabuchi is a professor of philosophy and the founding editor-in-chief of *Nnamdi Azikiwe Journal of Philosophy*, the Journal of the Department of Philosophy, Nnamdi Azikiwe University, Awka, Nigeria and the founding editor of *Essence: Interdisciplinary-International Journal of Philosophy*. His definition of politics depicts the happenings in many African countries, including Nigeria. The type of politics concerning this academic endeavour is the exercise of power in partisan politics and state governance.

From the above, it is obvious that politics involves state governance and how politicians secure their mandates from the electorate. However, this book is primarily concerned with the relationship between religion and politics in a heterogeneous society like Nigeria. Although there may occasionally be a need to assess state governance in an attempt to convey the objectives of this enterprise, for the most part the analysis will be restricted to the relationship between religion and politics.

Social Change

There is a need to initially define 'social' and 'change' separately before considering them together as a new hybrid noun 'social change'. Change is an act or process through which something becomes different, altered, or transformed (Simpkins et al., 2009: 30). The term 'social' has been used in several ways relating to society or its organizations or structures or people's behaviour. According to Max Weber, 'The primary meaning of "social"… is orientation to the behaviour of others' (Swedberg and Agevall 2005: 246). He explained further that 'action is "social" in so far as its subjective meaning takes account of the behaviour of others and is thereby oriented in its course' (Swedberg and Agevall 2005: 246).

When the two are combined and used together, they modify each other. Subsequently, the term 'social change' was defined by William Kornblum as follows:

The variations over time in the ecological ordering of populations and communities, in patterns of roles and social interactions, in the structure and functioning of institutions, and in the cultures of societies (2011: 566)

Social change is therefore defined as an extensive and multi-dimensional process involving virtually every aspects of social life. Therefore, it is precisely in this area that the concern of social change will become a point of discourse in this book.

Church

The word 'church' is commonly used among Christians, but it remains an arena of disagreements among them. This is because the word has several meanings and multiple usages, so it will be good to have an operating definition for the term. Hundreds of books discuss the meaning and origin of the word 'church'; however, a few will suffice to determine the operating definition for this book.

The word 'church' is English, translated from the Greek word *ekklesia*. However, according to Dewi A. Hughes and Matthew Bennett (1998: 72), the translation is incorrect. They argued that the 'church has a strong inclination to place, whereas *ekklesia* means a particular group of people gathered together—a congregation' (1998: 72). This postulation was supported by Dallas Burdette, who contended that the word *ekklesia* means a 'congregation or assembly' of people (2010: 416). Hughes and Bennett are suggesting that the term 'church' represents all adherents of Jesus Christ in a particular locality as in 1 Corinthians 1: 2, for example, the Anglican Communion, Church of Nigeria.

This could also mean a group of adherents coming together in a certain place to fellowship, such as house-church (Romans 16: 5; Colossians 4: 15). In the New Testament believers met in members' houses, as there were no buildings designated as churches.

According to Paul C. Jong, the word 'church' means the 'called out assembly', denoting 'God's people called out from the world and consecrated from the rest' (2008: 78). This same postulation was held by J. Rodman Williams. He said 'called out people' literally came from the Greek words *ek* (out) and *kaleo* (call) (Williams 1996: 27–30). So the word 'church' is also a corporate identity for those who believe and worship Jesus Christ, the whole body of believers, or the universal church, as in 1 Corinthians 12: 28.

The word *ekklesia* was used freely for gathering of citizens in the Ancient Athens at that time (Kerr 2011). It simply means a gathering of people summoned out by the trumpet of the herald to meet in a public place as an assembly for a particular purpose. This purpose could be civic, political, or other; it does not really have a connection with religion. The word over the years developed into a New Testament word and had acquired a new meaning completely different from what it used to be.

There is also the view championed by Kevin N. Giles that links the word *ekklesia* to an Old Testament background. He writes that *ekklesia* means 'assembly' or 'gathering' of the people of God and that it was deliberately chosen by Jesus Christ because of its resonance with the Old Testament meaning of the word (Giles 1995: 15). In the ancient Greek version of the Old Testament known as the Septuagint, the word *ekklesia* was often used to refer to Israel as the congregation of people called out by God (Enns 2008: 359) or God's people assembling in his presence (Goheen 2011: 161).

In other words, *ekklesia* was used in both the Old Testament and New Testament, but it was translated as 'assembly' in the Old Testament and as 'church' in the New Testament (Williams 2007: 16).

The definition of 'church' put forward by David W. Shenk and Ervin R. Sturtzman will be the most appropriate for this research project. They advocated that the 'church is the new community which brings healing to the divisions of humankind' (Shenk and Sturtzman 1988: 20). The healing referred to in the definition represents the dual nature of the church—both spiritual and social healing, which respectively address evangelistic and cultural mandates. George Raymond Hunsberger and Craig Van Gelder agree and assert that the church 'is an institution created by God that represents the presence and authority of God's reign on earth.' On the other hand, 'it is an organization constructed by humans for the purpose of living out a corporate life and mission' (1996: 285). It is this definition, in line with the dual nature and mandates, that will be used in this study regarding the church.

Development

Development has been defined by various scholars from different perspectives, each underlining their individual areas of speciality. Development could be either positive or negative, so it is a form of change. However, Mahbubul Haq, the prominent Pakistani economist and a founding pioneer of human development theory, offered a good description and detailed purpose of development. He states:

> The basic purpose of development is to enlarge people's choices. In principle, these choices can be infinite and can change over time. People often value achievements that do not show up at all, or not immediately, in income or growth figure; greater access to knowledge, better nutrition and health services, more secured livelihoods, security against crime and physical violence, satisfying leisure hours, political and cultural freedoms and sense of participation in community activities. The objective of development is to create an enabling environment for people to enjoy long, healthy and creative lives. (Adepoju et al., 2008: 205)

Haq's exposition is value-loaded and has human rights written all over it. According to Douglas J. Roche, 'development is the process that meets the needs and aspiration of the present without compromising the ability to meet those of the future' (1999: 72). This definition stresses economic growth, but at nobody's expense. Based on Haq's explanation of development, the UN developed a definition of development at its Millennium Summit in 2000 built on an agenda of eight goals, and this will be adopted as our operational definition for this academic endeavour (Adepoju et al., 2008: 205).

    Goal 1: Eradicate Extreme Hunger and Poverty
    Goal 2: Achieve Universal Primary Education
    Goal 3: Promote Gender Equality and Empower Women
    Goal 4: Reduce Child Mortality
    Goal 5: Improve Maternal Health
    Goal 6: Combat HIV/AIDS, Malaria, and Other Diseases
    Goal 7: Ensure Environmental Sustainability
    Goal 8: Develop a Global Partnership for Development

Development is about human betterment, economic opportunities, and social justice and it shall be seen from these perspectives in this book.

Society

Society as a term is relevant to this study and is generally associated with people's connection, interaction, participation, and partnership with one another within a particular geographical location. Like every other social structure, society has been defined in various ways, but Hairi Lasisi's definition will be employed in this study:

A society, or a human society, is a group of people related to each other through persistent relations, or a large social grouping sharing the same geographical or virtual territory, subject to the same political authority and dominant cultural expectations. Human societies are characterized by patterns of relationships (social relations) between individuals who share a distinctive culture and institutions; a given society may be described as the sum total of such relationships among its constituent members. (2012: 12)

The definition seems all-inclusive as society becomes an avenue that makes it possible for its members to benefit from the convergence in manners that would have been difficult for a solitary individual. There are lots of symbiosis relationships in a society as mentioned in the definition—hence its choice for this book.

Relations between Politics, Social Change, Church, Development, and Society

The five concepts (key words) introduced above are closely related and equally reinforcing. According to functional theory, 'all elements in a society are interrelated, and each contributes in some way to the attainment of both individual and collective goals' (Johnstone 1975: 132). Society is such that every individual is involved in one form of social relationship or the other, and in these relationships people share common interests and institutions. These institutions include but not limited to political parties and churches. These are established institutions and when they live up to the expectations of their members and the society they belong to, they work for development and social changes. On the other hand, when they fail to respond positively to the expectations of their members and the wider society, development and social change are affected. Generally, each element within society reacts to change in the other elements by adjusting.

Besides this, in any society power is either directly or indirectly shared amongst certain groupings. These groupings include political parties, religious groups (churches and other faiths), labour movements, cultural groupings, and manufacturers' associations, among many others. Each of these groups represents different interests, and they strive to protect those interests and serve them. Sometimes they form alliances to fight for a common cause, and at other times they work against each other as opponents. This probably is what Tony Bilton referred to as a 'pluralist diffusion model' (1981: 185). Politics and networking are always involved where groups are competing to acquire and control power, especially in a democratic society. In the process, each group is also involved in one development or the other to the society in order to outdo one another, to win support, or to retain power. This could be in response to the needs of the society or to placate a sector of the society. Whatever the reason, these developments will also cause social change to certain people within that society.

It is noteworthy that Christians, who are members of one church or the other, should be nurtured and discipled to impact society. The church teaches a high standard of morality and how to be good citizens of the state. Christianity has moral demands and consequences for those who accept Christ and his teachings. These are not simply personal moral codes but involve social mores; hence, morality and politics are profoundly fused together

The Mandates of the Church

for a Christian. Consequently, any attempt to explain the church's role without reference to reforming the morality of society is to deny the moral dimension of faith. The political activities of Christians such as William Wilberforce and Martin Luther King Jr. attest to this fact.

For meaningful developments and notable social change to occur in any society, there will have to be checks and balances in the system. The church could act as a check on the political class to stand up to correct, expose, and warn the government and keep it on the straight and narrow path of rectitude for the good of society (Mody 2003: 82). The political class, through the legislative arm of the government, also acts as a check and balance on the church and its members by making the laws that govern mutual living behaviours between the church, other faiths, and the wider society. So the church could be a strong opposition to the political class in the interest of the society. In so doing, there could be either positive or negative developments, depending on the response of the government.

The church is involved in politics locally and nationally. The church's doctrines express the Lordship of Jesus over the whole creation; this includes the political sphere, national and international relationships in the world. The church has been at the forefront of advocating for the weak, the poor, the widows, the outcast, protection of the environment, and social justice within the same political and social context with the wealthy, just like the prophet of the Old Testament. If politics is about power, then development is about equalizing the power dynamics. In all of these contexts, the politics of love and forgiveness cause social change and human development in the life of those directly affected in society.

The relationship between the church and the state (politics) at the collaborative level has led to positive developments for citizens and society in general. The church is involved in many areas of social life, such as the building of hospitals, schools, and libraries, as an employer of labour, assisting children, sick and elderly people, and prisoners. The church is touching people's lives and thereby causing social changes and human and economic developments in society. To be able to put many of social facilities in place, the church has to link up with local authorities, state governments, and other institutions in society.

Furthermore, the building of a strong, people-centred democracy is an important aspect of societal development. The active participation of the church as an established institution within society in this process enhances the dignity, development, transparency, and accountability of the democratic system. This requires the government's co-operation where and when necessary, while the church remains focused on keeping watch on the system, sensitizing the public, and championing the course of vulnerable citizens.

Theoretical Perspectives on Religion, Society, and Social Change

A theoretical perspective is a regular reflection of society that influences thinking and research. In a study of society or cultural phenomenon there will always be a need for theoretical explanations. According to sociology, many theories have emerged about societies and social behaviour both classical and contemporary. Nevertheless, there are three major traditional approaches in sociology, namely structural-functional, social conflict, and symbolic interaction theories. However, for this particular study, I will adopt and apply a hybrid of elements from these theories that affect the relationship between religion and social change to the case of the church in Lagos, Nigeria as an agent of social and political change in society.

Structural-Functional Theory

In structural-functional theory, which is also known as functionalism theory, society is viewed as a complex system whose parts work together to foster solidarity and stability (Macionis and Gerber 2010: 14). This method considers society from a macro-level perspective, that is, a general focus on the social structures that form the broad society. In other words, society developed in stages like living organisms (DeRosso 2003). This approach is concerned with the social structure of society, which is a relatively stable pattern of social behaviour, and the consequences of the action of the wholes society, which are termed 'social functions' (Andersen and Taylor 2007: 17–20). Emile Durkheim, the foremost proponent of this theory, stressed that 'all the individual parts of the structure are intimately connected and mutually dependent' (Bhowmick and Pramanick 2007: 64).

The main premise of this theory is that all societies have some basic needs that must be met by members of that society if it is to continue to exist. For this to be possible, Durkheim reasoned that in every society there is set of beliefs, common values, morals, and norms which are common to all members of that society (Eller 2007: 21). This he termed 'collective conscience', which Peter Hamilton termed 'collective origin' (Hamilton 1990: 356). It acts as a bond between the members of that society and gives them a sense or feeling of belonging (social solidarity), thereby shaping their behaviour (Jones

2001: 143). Functionalists believe that based on the 'collective conscience' and 'social solidarity' various parts of a society make contributions towards those needs. The main concern of functionalism is that these various parts function and interact together to stabilize and preserve the society and in the process develop steady progress to bring about significant and positive societal change.

Durkheim defined religion as a 'unified system of beliefs and practices relative to sacred thing' (2001: xxi). He says that religion is an integrative force in society because it has the power to shape collective beliefs (Andersen and Taylor 2012: 322). It offers stability in society by inspiring a sense of belonging and collective consciousness. He contends that religion provides quite a lot of functions in society and also relies on society for its survival, value, and significance, and vice versa (1893). He posits that religion provides and preserves social stability by eliminating tension that can possibly interrupt social order. Religion is viewed in a constructive institution, boosting harmonious living in society.

Social Conflict Theory

The social conflict theory highlights the role of force and power to achieve social order in society. According to Karl Marx, the chief proponent of the theory, every society is fragmented into groups, and all are competing for social and economic resources (Abu-Shakrah et al., 2005: 8). The privileged few with economic and political power and social resources dominate the rest of the society, using force and power to maintain social order in order to defend their benefits and status and thereby causing inequalities to persist.

This viewpoint is about the strong rich exploiting the weak poor by means of social control rather than by consensus. When inequalities exist within the society, power struggle is inevitable. This perspective emphasises class, race, and gender because they are the reasons for persistent struggles in society (Andersen and Taylor 2007: 22).

The main concern of this theory is highlighting the reasons for conflict in society and the ever-changing nature of society (Brockhaus 2005: 7). Unlike functionalism, which is about maintaining the status quo, eschewing social change, and depending on people's consensus to influence social order, social conflict theory challenges the status quo and inspires social change.

Marx regarded religion as a means of indoctrinating people to accept their current status in life, irrespective of their bad conditions of living, believing that rewards and happiness await them hereafter (Alexis 2010: 278). Hence, he declared that religion is the 'opium of the people' (Alexis 2010: 278). He viewed religion as an avenue for the rich to maintain their superior status over the poor and also as a means to prevent social change or social revolution by the oppressed in society.

Symbolic Interaction Theory

The symbolic interaction theory is about the meaning that people in society develop and rely upon in their day-to-day interactions. The theory examines society by focusing on the personal meanings that individuals impose on objects, events, and behaviours. According the principal proponents of the theory, Max Weber and George Herbert Mead, people behave based on what they believe and not just on what is objectively true (Andersen and Taylor 2007: 22). Therefore, society is said to be socially built around human interpretations (Andersen and Taylor 2012: 19). The interpretations of people's behaviours create the social bond. These interpretations are termed the 'definition of the situation' (Scott 2009: 24).

The symbolic interactionists' view of society is that people influence one another's everyday social interactions, and thus individuals create their own social world through their interactions (Ferrante 2010: 515). Fundamentally, social order is maintained through common understanding of everyday behaviour shared by the people. Interactionists posit that social change occurs when the positions and communication with one another change.

Through his research Weber discovered that religion can make an impact on social change. He wrote the *Protestant Ethic and the Spirit of Capitalism* (Weber 2003), where he seems to be arguing on two fronts. Ian Thompson writes:

> On the one hand, he seems to argue that Calvinism was a 'causal' factor in the development of a capitalist spirit – it was a very active force in promoting social change. On the other hand, there is the idea that Calvinism and spirit of capitalism were very close – the ideas were in close harmony. (1986: 42)

Calvinism was a doctrine followed by those who believed in the religious doctrine of John Calvin, which maintains that salvation comes through faith in God and also that God has already chosen those who will believe and be saved (termed 'elective affinity' by Weber) (Swedberg and Agevall 2005: 83). This group valued working for money and reinvesting the profits back into their businesses, so as to guarantee continuous functioning businesses, expansion, and eventually industrialisation. He argues that the religious belief of accumulation by this group matches the ethos of capitalism (Edmonds 2002: 9). The point Weber seems to be making here is that the rise of capitalism could cause social change in society. Religious beliefs influence people's behaviours. He studied religion on a large scale around the globe, including Ancient Judaism, Christianity, Hinduism, Buddhism, and Taoism, before arriving at the conclusion that social change is predicated on people's religious beliefs.

The 'It Depends' Approach

Giving the prevailing situations in most societies, these theories are evidently occurring concurrently in many nations, they are not exclusive of one another. On religion's part, since two of the three theories view religion as constructive, harmonious living boosting and status quo maintaining institution within the society and the third theory views it as a catalyst for change in the society, then, there is a need for a hybrid approach that will accommodate the three theories. The hybrid model (It depends approach) represents the not too obvious change elements inherent in the first two theories and the very obvious change elements in the third theory. In other words, the hybrid approach is an attempt to blend the three theories in regards to these views on religion and society.

The arguments regarding the connection between religion and social change are undoubtedly complex. From the above, Durkheim and Marx argued that religion helps to preserve the prevailing status quo in any society and provides an explanation and justification for social orders. However, Marx's social conflict theory could be used to challenge the status quo and inspire social change. For example, the fact that religion promises a better world hereafter could potentially raise people's consciousness and lead to a social revolution (Thompson 1986: 43). Hence, religion can be an agent of change or stability (Roberts and Yamane 2011: 318).

However, the most tenable perception for this particular study is Weber's perception. Weber argued that religion could trigger social change, depending on certain factors. These factors, as introduced by Ian Thompson in his book *Sociology in Focus: Religion,* can affect what impact religion has within a given society at a particular time. These factors are described in the next section.

Factors Affecting Religion's Impact on Society

Charismatic Leaders

Weber outlined the power of charisma in producing social change. He argued that it is 'the specifically creative revolutionary force of history' (Weber 1978: 1117). On the one hand, charismatic leaders are usually religious leaders who are not pleased with the situation of the society or community they find themselves in and reason that they are capable of providing a rallying point for despondency with a conviction about a better tomorrow. Examples are Martin Luther King, John Wesley, Winston Churchill, Adolph Hitler, Mahatma Gandhi, Ayatollah Khomeini, Mother Teresa, Bishop Desmond Tutu, Bill Clinton, and Mother Teresa.

On the other hand, the phrase 'charismatic' stems from *charismata pneumatika*, meaning 'gifts of the Spirit' as used by Apostle Paul in 1 Corinthians 12–14. The term refers to believers who exhibit unusual divine grace or anointing of the Holy Spirit. Therefore, charismatic leaders from Christians' point of view are those leaders who are functioning and manifesting the extraordinary divine anointing gifts of the Holy Spirit. A few examples from Nigeria include Pastor E. A. Adeboye, the late Archbishop Benson Idahosa, Bishop David Oyedepo, Pastor W. F. Kumuyi, Pastor Tunde Bakare, Archbishop Joseph A. Adetiloye, and Bishop Mike Okonkwo.

Belief and Practices

While some religious beliefs and practices can lead to social change, others may see change as unnecessary or unlikely. According to Meredith McGuire, the belief system held by a religion will shape its role in society (McGuire 2002: 242). If a religious sect believes that societal conditions need no improvement, that it is the 'will of God' for things to remain as they are, then there will be no need for such a group to participate in any pressure to effect social changes in the polity. Examples are Jehovah Witnesses, 'New Order' (the Millennium), New Age (individualistic spirituality) and Hinduism (reincarnation and caste).

Relationship to Society

This has to do with the type of familiarity that exists between religion and the state. The closer the faith (religion) is to the government (state), the less likelihood of posing any pressure for social change, whereas, if the 'church' is independent of the state, the pressure for certain social change is expected. For example, Church of England is linked to the state (Fahlbusch 2008: 191). The Roman Catholic church in Lithuania in 1990 demanded independence in Latvia, Lithuania, and Estonia, and church bells signalled demonstrations (Birzulis 2013). In Nigeria, however, no particular religion or sect has a grip on the state, but the people are more loyal to their religion than to the state. Consequently, the people respect their religious leaders more than secular leaders (Falola 2001: 10).

It is also possible that some religious movements can pave the way for social change, especially when they are on the fringes of society and membership primarily consists of poor and disadvantaged people. A good example is the 'millenarian movements' (Thompson 1986: 43). The term is a wide-embracing classification for varieties of anti-colonial protest in the Third World (Trompf 1990: 28). These are voluntary groups whose followers are often from the oppressed, alienated, deprived, and idealistic communities within the lowest cadre of society. According Friedrich Engels, they are often pre-political groups, whose ideas and beliefs metamorphose into full political groups (Thompson 1986: 43). Examples from Nigeria include the Egbe Omo Oduduwa, later the Action Group AG, and the Nigerian Youth Movement (NYM), later the National Council of Nigeria and Cameroon still later renamed as the National Council of Nigerian Citizens (NCNC).

Social Status of Religious Membership

It is possible that established religious organisations draw some of their members from the higher echelons of society and high-ranking government officials, while sectarian movements attract less privileged people in society. It is therefore easier for the sectarian movements to use their members as machinery for the promotion of social change (Buckser 1996: 148).

The Presence of Alternative Avenues to Change

When there is no political platform to achieve necessary social change, religion may likely be the next port of call as a structured institution with the wherewithal to bring about the desired social change (Thompson 1986: 47). According to Otto Maduro, 'religion is not necessarily a functional, reproductive or conservative factor in society: it is often one of the main (and sometimes the only) available channel to bring about a social revolution' (O'Toole 1984: 192). Although both Durkheim (functionalism) and Marx (symbolic interaction) explained possible roles of religion in society as either a conservative force or an initiator of social change, Otto Maduro differs from the above line of argument. He argues that religion does not act as a conservative force, but rather as a radical force, a drive for change.

The neo-Marxists, the group to which Maduro belongs, are critical of such narrow views that see religion as conservative. Maduro posited that religion has the potential to inspire revolutionary change in any society. He argues that the lack of outlets for grievances made the church and its ministers the last hope of the common man. To some extent Maduro and company might be right, considering the activities and effects of the Boko-Haram insurgence in Northern Nigeria. However, that does not take away the fact that religion is also a conservative force that helps to maintain social stability and harmony in society.

It is important to point out that the roles religion assumes in any society depend on that particular society, the type of religion in question, and the relationship of that religion to society.

Organisational Structure

An organised religion with organisational structures has considerable influence on its members' focus and purpose. Established churches are in this category and as such are often used as tools to prevent change (Emerson 2000: 138). However, if a religious organisation has all these qualities and is independent of the state and is well funded either from within or without, it can oppose the authorities and criticise the existing social and political arrangements.

Overall, the church can be an agent of social and political change given certain factors. The absence of other avenues for change in any society leaves religion with no choice other than to act the important role of change agent. Moreover, if religion's beliefs are crucial to the people and form a central part of the culture of any society, then religion has considerable ability to change society. However, the availability of various avenues for social change implies religion may assume a marginal role and may be confined to just its conservative role.

Chapter Four

Biblical Reflections on Church and Social Involvement

When we struggle for human rights, for freedom, for dignity, when we feel that it is a ministry of the church to concern itself for those who are hungry, for those who have no schools, for those who are deprived, we are not departing from God's promise. He comes to free us from sin, and the church knows that sin's consequences are all such injustices and abuses. The church knows it is saving the world when it undertakes to speak also of such things.

— *Oscar A. Romero,*
The Violence of Love

The church is one of the stakeholders in any society where churches exist and remain in high statistical proportion to the population. The supporters of the two mandates of the church, as pointed out in earlier chapters, are of the opinion that the church was commissioned to proclaim not just the gospel of redemption and disciplining converts but was equally called and authorised to improve society. They claimed that the church must be concerned to create a just society and should be distinguished as different, exemplary, and remarkable through self-sacrificing service to humanity. Evangelism is about bringing people to Christ, to teach, train, and equip them so that they can transform and shape society (the cultural mandate) for the benefit of everybody. To them, the Great Commission (evangelism) is on a par with the cultural mandate and the church can only fulfil its mission by recognising and undertaking the two together. Nancy Pearcey and others are of the opinion that, biblically, the church is not living up to its responsibility as the representative of Christ in society if it is not socially involved. Therefore, we need to know those biblical bases for the church's social involvement and must do some biblical exegesis where necessary.

The Old Testament

As far as the cultural mandate of the church is concerned, the Old Testament is replete with God's interest in the welfare of the people, especially those at the lowest end of the social ladder. The basic moral test is how most of the widows, orphans, and other defenceless or disadvantaged in society are faring. Our society is inherently unjust, and the gap between rich and poor is widening on daily basis. However, biblical Christians and the church are instructed to put the needs of the poor and weak first. The following scriptural verses are biblical testimonies to this fact: Exodus 22: 20–26; Leviticus 19: 9–10, 15, 23: 22, 25: 35; Deuteronomy 15: 11, 16: 20; Job

34: 2–28; Psalm 82: 2–4; Proverb 29: 7, 31: 8–9; Isaiah 1: 6–19, 10: 1–2, 25: 4–5, 58: 4–11; Jeremiah 7: 5–7, 22: 3, 13–16, 29: 4–7; Amos 5: 11–15, 21–24; Micah. 6:8; and Zechariah 7: 9–10.

The Old Testament prophets are full of assertions about the accountability of nations to God, the creator of the universe, who is able to raise nations and cast nations down (Zechariah 12: 1–7). The prophets, as instructed by God, commended nations for doing good, and where the opposite was the case, they were criticized for wrongdoings. Although, there were no churches then, the prophets represented God in that dispensation just as the church is also representing God now. It is very instructive to note that much of the content of the prophets' messages to rulers was about social justice, speaking up for those that cannot speak for themselves (Proverbs 31: 8). This in itself is a political dynamite and Francis Chan believes it is still possible and relevant in this modern context. Speaking about the poor in our midst, Chan wrote:

> Much of their (the poor) daily hardship and suffering could be relieved with access to food, clean water, clothing, adequate shelter, or basic medical attention. I believe that God wants His people, the church, to meet these needs. (2008: 119)

Matthew Goheen and Craig Bartholomew (Bartholomew 2008: 66) also concur. They believe that the church has to be involved in every aspect of God's creations, including society and social issues, so as to preserve the cultural mandate and be God's true representative on earth.

The Bible talks of God's creation and His relationship with all that were created. He desires justice and fairness should reign amongst all. He sends the Old Testament prophets to individuals just like he did to nations, warning them of disastrous consequences of their injustices to fellow human beings. A good example is the Prophet Nathan to King David (2 Samuel 12: 1–12). Others prophets such as Elijah, Elisha, Isaiah, Amos, and Jeremiah were at one time or another sent to either individuals or state leaders by God to challenge them about their social deeds. Thus, if the Old Testament prophets were indeed God's representatives speaking out against social ills as caused by the corporate sin of communities, cities, and nations and the personal sin of individuals, then the Old Testament supports the social involvement of the church (God's representative) in our societies.

On political involvement, it is on record that Joseph was a prime minister and he exercised civil powers in Egypt (Genesis 41: 40–57). Likewise, Daniel rose to the summits of civil power in Babylon, and the nation benefited during his reign (Daniel 6: 3).

The New Testament

The different accounts in the New Testament that point to both individual Christians and the church getting involved in social issues are too numerous to check one after the other. However, some passages will be given, and some will be analysed to dissect what the scripture was actually passing across to its reader. The following scriptural verses are biblical testimonies to this fact: Matthew 5: 9, 21–24, 6: 25–34; Luke 4: 16–21, 16: 19–31; John 4: 1–42, 15: 12–17; Acts 2: 43–47, 4: 32–35; Romans 1: 20, 12: 4–8, 9–18, 13: 8–10; I Cor. 10: 26, 12:

The Mandates of the Church

12–26; II Cor. 9: 6–15; Hebrews 10: 24–25; Colossians 3: 9–17; James 2: 1–8, 14–18; I Peter 4: 8–11; I John 3: 1–2, 16–18 and 4: 7–12, 19–21.

If one takes a closer look at many of the above scriptures, one will discover that they are teachings about Christians' responsibilities to fellow Christians and not particularly to those outside of the church. They are encouraging Christians to offer practical help to those in need within the Christian community, although the account of Acts 9: 36–39 is an exception to this pattern. It was recorded that Dorcas helped people beyond the church setting. She affected lives within and outside the church. Meanwhile, there were instances where the organized church was involved in meeting the needs of the poor, the less privileged, or those who had social problems as a result of their faith (2 Cor. 8: 1–9; 15-16). These examples of help were given to the 'saints', not to the general society.

Consequently, the scriptures quoted above do not address the question of the basis of the church's involvement in society. If the church is basing its argument or reasons for getting involved in societal problems or social welfare solely on most of the above scriptures, then the argument is weak, as there are distinctions between the Christians within the church and the general society. However, Galatians 6: 10 is a better premise for the church to get involved in society, as it is more inclusive of the general populace. Our love is intended for all people with an eternal view toward evangelism in all of our actions.

The Ministry of Jesus

The activities, proclamations, and relationships of Jesus Christ during His earthly ministry as recorded in the

New Testament are enough reasons for the involvement of the church in our society. The New Testament also asserts God's love for humanity and concern for justice; these are the premises upon which Jesus's ministry was based.

Proclamations

Jesus announced His mission in His first public message in the synagogue in Nazareth. He read from the prophet Isaiah 61: 1–2.

> The Spirit of the Lord is on me, because he has anointed me to preach good news to the poor. He has sent me to proclaim freedom for the prisoners and recovery of sight for the blind, to release the oppressed, to proclaim the year of the Lord's favour (Luke 4: 18-19).

His mission from this scripture is both social and evangelical. The poor need help beyond what the world can give. His ministry was to proclaim liberation from sin and all its consequences. In other words, His mission was preaching and healing (spiritually and physically) to meet every human need. His style pours contempt on all human greatness, and seeks, like God, to do good to those whom the world neglects or despises (1 Corinthians 1: 26–30). His ministry was distinguished by sensitivity to the weak, helpless, oppressed, and maligned people in society.

Jesus said that His disciples are the salt and the light to the world.

> You are the salt of the earth. But if the salt loses its saltiness, how can it be made salty again? It is no longer good for anything, except to be thrown out and trampled underfoot. You

are the light of the world. A town built on a hill cannot be hidden. Neither do people light a lamp and put it under a bowl. Instead they put it on its stand, and it gives light to everyone in the house. In the same way, let your light shine before others, that they may see your good deeds and glorify your Father in heaven. (Matthew 5: 13–16)

He refers to Christians' roles and responsibilities in the world. He likens Christians to salt and by extension likens the church to salt. Salt, depending on the context, can be a food preservative or a taste enhancer for insipid food; to do either of these, it purifies and penetrates into the food. I presume the salt in this context is a seasoning agent. As Keith Krell noted, Jesus's mention of the taste of salt supports this interpretation (Krell). The church and Christians generally are preservatives to any society in which they might find themselves, preserving it from the wickedness inherent in that society. They can bring flavour into politics, economics, culture, and the environment. The church needs to spread salt all over our society through its social welfare agenda and by its encouragement of individual Christians to penetrate their society with righteous deeds and save it from moral putrescence and decay. Unfortunately, in many parts of the world today the church is withdrawing from culture, thereby handing over the management and control of society to the unrighteous. 'When the righteous are in authority, the people rejoice: but when the wicked bears rule, the people mourn'(Proverbs 29: 2 KJV). Krell opined that 'When Christians pulled out of public education, politics, and the media, righteous decisions left with them' (Krell). How does the Christian community (the church and Christians) contribute to the development of culture, moral principles, and social life, and how does it add value to society when it withdraws into its shell?

In addition to the earlier salt analogy, Jesus likens His disciples to light. The presence of light in darkness is unambiguous. The presence of the church vis-à-vis Christians in the world should be like a light in the darkness with shining examples of good deeds that must be evident for all to see. It means the Christian community has to be a light for all the people of the world; hence, there is no restriction of good deeds to fellow Christians alone. As disciples of Jesus Christ, it is not enough to have private personal holiness; we must also have public exposure (France 2007: 176). Jesus notes that nothing can remain hidden or secret. In fact, the task of the Christian community is to be light-bearers of Christ so that others may see the truth of the gospel and be freed from the impetuousness of sin and deception.

In addition, Jesus said, 'You shall love your neighbour as yourself' (Mark 12: 31 NKJV). The question that would readily come to anybody's mind after reading this scripture is 'Who is my neighbour?' I honestly believe Jesus meant it to include all mankind—even our enemies! To support this, Jesus told His disciples about that well-known parable of the Good Samaritan, making it evident that to 'love your neighbour' means to love all persons, everywhere. This story succinctly demonstrates how we can show love for others. Therefore, if the disciples (the Christian Community) love everyone, then it will be a disservice and disobedient to the commandment of Jesus not be concerned or involved with society.

Mark 10: 45 provides the climax: 'For even the Son of Man did not come to be served, but to serve, and to give His life as a ransom for many.' The biblical backdrop for social welfare activities of the church shows Jesus's love and commitment to service toward humanity. It is impossible to understand God's love if one is isolated from the society where one lives. His love is expressed to individuals and society alike. Therefore, if the church and its adherents obey Jesus' command to 'love God,' 'love one another,' and 'love your neighbour,' then God's love for the whole society and His desire to reform it must be considered and giving a pride of place in the church's tasks.

Activities

The gospel accounts showed that Jesus was not a politician. He was not involved with the politicians and did not belong to any political party. However, certain statements and activities of Jesus Christ were heavily toned with civic awareness and deliberate deviation from the status quo.

He never attempted to sidestep public controversy, especially when it concerned the word of God. The Bible's account in Matthew 19: 8 is a good example. When He was asked about the issue of divorce, He replied, 'Moses permitted you to divorce your wives because your hearts were hard. But it was not this way from the beginning.' Considering the situation as at that time, Jesus's position was as controversial as the issue involved. The fact is that there were two main schools of thought on the issue of divorce at that time (Deuteronomy 24: 1–4), and Jesus took side with one over the other and yet pointed back to God's original idea for marriage (Genesis 1: 27; 2: 24).

Apart from being a controversial subject, the topic was as much political as it is social. At that period Jewish men were divorcing their Jewish wives on the flimsiest excuses so that they could marry gentile women (v. 9-11) for what Gavison-Medan termed 'cultural-national reason' (S. Weiss 2013: 193), that is, in anticipation of political gains and benefits that might arise if the Jewish state ceased to exist and leadership revert to gentile families. The Jews who had intermarried into those families would benefit (Efird 2001: 41). Yet Jesus made His opinion known without fear or favour.

He did not abstain from making political statement or taking political action. First, a political trap was set up for Jesus concerning the payment of tax to the Roman government. At the time there was great acrimony on the part of the Jews against the Roman government for asking them to pay tribute money to the emperor and because of general Roman nosiness in Jewish life. So it was a political question, and Jesus did not dodge it. Then Jesus said to them, 'Give back to Caesar what is Caesar's and to God what is God's.' And they were amazed at Him (Mark 12: 17). They were amazed with His answer because He was able to avoid their trap and at the same time found a way to teach a religious lesson—that there are obligations to the state that do not encroach on our Christian obligations to God.

Second, either knowingly or unknowingly His choice of disciples had political undertones. Matthew was a tax collector and Simon, a Zealot. The Zealots were a first-century political sect among the Judean Jews who wanted to topple the ruling Roman government (Efird 1980: 21).

Third, the narrative of the Cleansing of the Temple by Jesus (recorded in John 2: 14–17 at the beginning of Jesus's ministry and in all other gospels towards the end of His ministry) is seen as a threat to religious leaders and the temple authority, particularly Caiaphas, the high priest. To them, His bold action meant that he was laying claim over their enterprise (the temple), and this set the stage for their conflict (Pilgrim 1999: 98). He challenged the financial institution of the sacrificial system during one of their biggest festivals, the Passover (Metzger 2010: 287). This was not just action but also made both a political and religious statement. He was seen as a traitor to the nationalist cause by the Jewish leader (Borg 1984: 6).

Jesus was not afraid to go against customs and traditions. He healed on the Sabbath, and the Pharisees complained (Mark 3: 1—6). The Sabbath law is as much a religious issue as it is a national issue to the Jewish people. The Pharisees as the custodians of the law were vengefully looking for an opportunity to publicly disgrace Jesus based on their previous exchanges and tensions that had built up between themselves and Jesus. He was not ready to please them at the expense of His mission (Luke 4: 18–19). The narrative of how He healed the man with a withered hand in a synagogue on a Sabbath showed His overriding compassion for the sick, and thinking that they could trap Him with it, He was challenged for not keeping the Sabbath law, but He defended His actions and His line of argument left the Pharisees speechless and laid bare their ulterior motives.

Association

Jesus strongly associated Himself with the poor, the disadvantaged, the social outcasts, the sick, the morally reprobate, and the political outcasts such as the tax collectors and Zealots. People were shocked that Jesus would want to associate with outcasts and sinners, but He kept to the script of His mission, which was targeted at the lost. So, His mission was not limited to a particular race but was a global assignment. He was socially involved with the outcasts and downtrodden. He identified with them and cared for them because they could not get help anywhere else. He fed the hungry, healed the sick, and yet ministered to those who needed His help in order to find God. He fulfilled both the evangelism and cultural mandates in His association with people. Hence, the instruction He gave His disciples was as follows:

> 'Go therefore and make disciples of all the nations, baptizing them in the name of the Father and the Son and the Holy Spirit, teaching them to observe all that I commanded you; and lo, I am with you always, even to the end of the age.' (Matthew 28: 18–20 NKJV)

Put simply, Jesus was very much aware of His environment politically, socially, and culturally, and this was reflected in His teachings, associations, and activities.

In conclusion, it is important to build a robust society, develop a people-centred democracy, and offer good governance for the whole country while taking into account the importance of religion and politics to the people in the society. From the above arguments, the objective of this book is echoed from both religious and philosophic perspectives that the church and the state are interrelated and are both necessary for society. They are social phenomena that cannot be divorced from each other.

However, it is pertinent to note that the role of the church in the state and vice-versa could be restricted by individual preferences, doctrinal dispositions, government policies, and the composition of society. None the less,

The Mandates of the Church

they will keep on influencing each other. In a secular state like Nigeria, if the church and other faiths play their roles as expected of them, society will be better for it. If the two independent institutions are genuinely concerned about the well-being of the populace, then, the church and the state could have a meaningful and successful interactive relationship. Society at large stands to benefit from such a relationship if both sides play their roles legitimately without one becoming the appendage of the other.

Chapter Five

The 'How' of the Church's Engagement in Society

At the end of life we will not be judged by how many diplomas we have received, how much money we have made, how many great things we have done. We will be judged by "I was hungry, and you gave me something to eat, I was naked and you clothed me. I was homeless, and you took me in.

— *Mother Teresa*

Contrary to the common belief that Christian churches do not have much to offer society apart from spiritual guidance and the general well-being of those within its constituency, there are a number of ways in which the church can engage the state to the benefit of all and sundry. Also, there are approaches the church can adopt so that it can succour the populace both socially and politically. The fact is that the church's social and political actions are means of fulfilling its mission—its responsibilities to God, society, and humanity. However, it seems that many Christian churches have neglected socio-political involvement and considered it as no-go area for the church, forgetting that the mission of the church transcends its boundary and extends into society. Maybe the story will change if the church knows how best it can engage the state and in what manner it could be socially and politically involved in society without losing its spiritual focus and values. Moreover, its involvement could actually attract a lot of new members into the body—channels of evangelism.

The church must be aware of its responsibilities to God and society before either getting involved or not getting involved in the state's affairs. If it must get involved, it is imperative that it responds to social and political problems biblically and correctly. There are certain features that it needs to take into consideration before it can meaningfully engage the system articulately and these features, could also be used as guiding dynamics in its response to any of the societal problems.

Living as an Example of God's Kingdom

The church must learn to live by the scripture; by doing so, it is leading by example. It must put its house in order to mirror God's household and principles. The primary drive for the church's involvement in the state is centred on the need and search for an egalitarian society where peace, love, justice, compassion, etiquette, community, belonging, dialogue, participation, and equality are endorsed and maintained. Hence, it has to demonstrate these attributes from within by living out the faith. Without doubt the church will become a challenge to the rest of the society; only then can it effectively challenge the social or political structures of the state.

Speaking on behalf of the oppressed in society will be meaningless if the church cannot uphold justice within its members or show compassion to the needy within its fold. The church must demonstrate the reality of forgiveness and love, renouncing greed and egoism, and must show how to live together beyond the barriers of class, education, wealth, race, position, or any other such factors that trigger division between people in society. These virtues have to permeate the society from within the church; otherwise it would be seen as hypocritical. Rowan Williams posited that the church is 'the place where the rationale of all other relations is made plain and their deepening and securing made possible' (2000: 220). In other words, the church is a place where justification for interactions is visible and understandable to all parties.

Prophetic Responsibility

The responsibility of the church is not limited to an evangelical mandate; it also has a cultural mandate, which incorporates its prophetic obligation to society. These mandates are not exclusive of each other but are rather complementing each other. Therefore, for the church's mission to be comprehensive, it must continue in this prophetic tradition of the Old Testament; that is, it will serve as the voice of the voiceless, instigating leaders to have a rethink on issues, causing persons in charge to do the right things, and advocating justice and righteousness in the polity. One of the major messages of the Old Testament prophets is social justice, which is still very much relevant in society today—hence the need to follow this pattern.

Jesus Christ could also be regarded as a prophetic social critic, who criticized social injustices, leadership oppression, and religious hypocrisy in His time. He drew a parallel between the commission with which the Father had sent Him into the world and the way He was sending us as disciples (John 20: 21). Hence, part of the church's responsibility is to criticize sinful deeds and wicked policy ideas and to deconstruct unjust systems and structures in society by speaking out against them. The church cannot just be picking up the victims of these injustices; it needs to address the power behind the injustice in society.

This is likely to make the church politically significant and put it in sensitive positions that could result in a catalyst of change within the state's structures and society at large. Though Stephen Carter agrees that the church has a prophetic role to play in society, he was none the less quick to caution that it must abstain from partisan politics (2000: 175). He probably sounded this note of warning so that the church does not get its 'hands soiled' in the game of politics, and this is where religious lobbyists come in. This will give the church boldness to enter the public fray purified at any time, as a prophetic voice calling the state to account for its wrongs (Carter 2000: 113).

Development of a Contextual Theology for Good Governance

In view of the situation in Nigeria, the socio-economic laxity, the religious complexity, and the political conundrum, the church might need to develop a contextual theology to guide its involvement in the socio-political life of the state. A well-defined theological foundation will act as a compass that guides its involvement in the affairs of the state, and it will also help the church to establish boundaries depending on the prevailing situation. This will reflect its biblical views, Christian worldviews, and socio-political analysis of the state's circumstances within the Nigerian context. If this is done, it will enable the church to engage the government in a more robust manner. Moreover, it will be a ready answer to anyone that dares challenge its participation either socially or politically in affairs of the state.

Maximizing Potentials and Resources

Considering the numerous problems in Nigeria, the church is limited to attending to almost all aspects of the socio-political challenges, since it is on its own. It is therefore wise to prioritize its involvement by maximizing its potentials and resources. This can only be achieved by concentrating on specific socio-political issues that it can handle effectively and leaving others to the other religious groups within the state. By trying to attend to many issues concurrently, it might not be effective and efficient in many of them, and there is also the tendency to make mistakes.

Moreover, it might be straining the members too much in terms of time, commitment, and funds if it tries to finance many projects simultaneously. With no external financing or financial support, it is only logical for the church to maximize the available funds on fewer projects. However, partnering and collaborating across Christian denominations or organizations committed to a common cause could make the contributions of the church more effective to society. Through cooperation and networking, it can arguably increase its coverage and quality of service delivery with less effort. Also, there is likely going to be improved utilization of both human and financial resources.

Political Areas
Tackling Corruption in the Polity

In the case of corruption, a more robust approach needs to be adopted. The individual churches cannot confront it all alone either on the state or national level. Therefore, to be able to help in this area, it would be better if the various denominations could team up with the national body representing all churches in Nigeria, the Christian Association of Nigeria (CAN). Together they can put together methods through which government officials, especially Christians, will be made accountable to the people they are serving. After all, 'with responsibility comes accountability' (Bill et al., 2004: 84). They might even need to collaborate with civic agencies that are known for fighting against corruption. Agencies such as Transparency International, Economic and Financial Crimes Commission (EFCC), Independent Corrupt Practices Commission (ICPC), and other anti-corruption agencies both home and abroad could be used either to curb or stamp out corruption. Once the Christians or the church start, the Muslims will in no time follow suit. After all, a good percentage of the leaders and politicians are either Christians or Muslims.

Engaging Professional Lobbyists

This approach can help the church get indirectly involved in the politics of the state via policy making without being confrontational. It will ensure that its concerns and those of other religious citizens are translated into political policy for the benefit of all. It will afford the church the opportunity to be represented by a professional lobbyist or lobbyist organisation that can convince members of the state executive council or the legislative arm of government to enact policies that will reflect its wishes.

Presently, there is just a little evidence to suggest the involvement or influence of the church in policy formulation and implementation in Nigeria. The lobbying profession, though not yet pronounced in Nigeria generally, is none the less a recognised legitimate and integral part of the democratic process (Joo-Cheong 2010: 247). The task of a professional lobbyist is not limited to swaying legislators to favour a particular policy; it includes studying and analysing legislation, attending congresses, and enlightening government officials, corporate bodies, and other interest groups on significant and relevant issues. The lobbyist also attempts to win over opinion leaders and the general public through assertive publicity (Woodstock Theological Centre 2002: 82–89).

There are lobbyists for various interest groups and institutions. Some specialize in religious matters; hence, they are referred to as religious lobbyists. According to Robert Booth Fowler (2010: 293) and Daniel J. B. Hoffrenning (1995: 71) lobbyists are important aspects of democracy, ensuring representation by congressmen and senators of their peoples' views. In Nigeria this could be of help, and if the church does provide lobbyists, they would need to assess their political stance and not appear politically biased. Rather, they would need to hold the moral ground on biblical bases of ethics. This is further explained in the next section below. With this unique position of religious lobbyists, the church can lessen its direct involvement in political issues and concentrate on its social involvement with society. This will help the church to focus on other things of equal importance and relieve itself of the argument of whether it is right or not for a church to be politically involved in society.

Public Enlightenment

The church is primarily a place for teaching about the gospel of Jesus Christ, but it is also a place where people are educating and are educated about a number of other issues relating to human development and social cohesion, including their civic responsibilities to the state and to other citizens. Many of Nigeria's foremost nationalists—the likes of Nnamdi Azikiwe, Herbert Macaulay, Obafemi Awolowo, and a host of others—were taught and learnt honesty, dependability, fear of God, trustworthiness, love and togetherness, leadership, and political virtues from the church. These are rare subjects these days either in public or spiritual gatherings. However, God is still interested in raising men that will change the world. Therefore, as long as God is interested in transforming a man, he is also interested in transforming the human society in which that man lives. Consequently, the onus falls on the church to develop men who will be able to stand up for the right societal values. With this type of grass roots enlightenment, accountability will not be difficult if these men find themselves in positions of power later.

The church could also be a facilitator of forums where those outside the church can be informed about public policies. A good example is the case of the Diocese of Lagos West, Anglican Communion, Church of Nigeria. This church has been organising debates for gubernatorial elections in Lagos State, Nigeria for the past twelve years (2003, 2007, 2011, and 2015). The debates were organised so that the church, its members, and the general public could have interactive sessions with the gubernatorial candidates in the state. They presented their resumes, their political parties' philosophies, and their personal manifestoes to the audience on how the state can be developed and moved forward for the benefit of the populace. The audience later asked them salient questions concerning the present and the future of the state and the nation. All events were well attended by many politicians from various political parties across the state, as well as members of various churches and other faiths within the state. With events such as this, the electorate can make informed choices.

The DLW also set up a Sensitization and Observation Committee (SOC) for each of the elections. This group was saddled with the responsibility of sensitizing the public and Christians in particular about their civic responsibilities towards the state and the nation at the election. The group was also officially registered and accredited with the Independence National Electoral Commission (INEC), so as to observe the actual elections, voter turnout, and the general conduct of the process.

This is an uncommon area for churches in Nigeria to participate in, but it added value to the conduct of the elections, particularly in Lagos State. The DLW was able to commend the electoral body where necessary and advise and give suggestions to the body where lapses were observed, so that there may be improvement in subsequent elections in the state and the nation as a whole.

Leadership

The church should be committed to giving exemplary leadership within the household of faith first and foremost by exhibiting the principle of sacrificial service, exercising

The Mandates of the Church

leadership as servanthood and power in service to God and humanity. If the leaders in Christian churches can be shining examples in character, words, and deeds when compared to the style and system of the secular leaders, there is every likelihood that the church and its leadership will command increasing respect and recognition from both the state and the populace. Moreover, such an impeccable leader will be able to be a 'watchman' for the populace. He cries out where and when necessary for the benefit of everybody. However, he doesn't just criticise; he offers practicable and credible suggestions as alternatives. Constructive criticism is not judgment of the government or its efforts; it is censure for the manner in which things are done, so that other options or better alternatives can be considered. The government requires criticism to perform well (Falola 2003: 253).

This was seen recently (January 2010) in Nigeria when a pastor convened a group of eminent Nigerians and led them on a peaceful protest to demand a more responsive and accountable leadership on the one hand and on the other installing the then vice-president of Nigeria as acting president pending the outcome of the medical treatment of the actual president. Pastor Tunde Bakare of Latter Rain Assembly was able to pull people like Nobel laureate Wole Soyinka, Femi Falana (SAN), Ayo Obe, Uche Onyeagucha, Auwal Musa-Rafsanjani, and many others for this noble cause because he has exhibited the principle of sacrificial service. He had exercised leadership as servanthood and power in service to God and humanity over the years. He has been consistent as a Christian leader and prophet to the nation, criticizing the state's unjust policies and structures inherent in the system and commending them when they get it right. Hence, his words are weighty in society and his opinion cannot be easily waved aside.

Social Areas

Constitutionally, it is the responsibility of the state to cater for its citizens irrespective of creed, race, or social status. The provision of basic amenities of life is within the purview of the state; however, many states have failed in this regard due to a number of factors. In some instances where these amenities were provided, they were either substandard or unaffordable for the poor and the needy among the populace. Consequently, there are gaps that need to be plugged—hence the need for the church to activate its cultural mandate and help address all issues that affect mankind and human society. According to Ade Odumuyiwa, Christian churches should not be limited to spiritual exercises, but they need to participate in governance and development of people and community. He underlined possible areas of participation of the church (2013: 211):

- Humanitarian services
- Educational development
- Employment generation
- Social and ethical development
- Governance by example
- Improved economy
- Spiritual and moral development

The list is not exhaustive; nevertheless, each local church or individual Christian church has to take certain factors into consideration before embarking on any of the possible areas of services identified above. These factors include but not limited to the following:

The Mandates of the Church

- Areas of priority
- Necessary needs lacking within its environment at that point in time
- Availability and affordability of human resources
- Available resources and financial capacity of the church
- Level of involvement

This sort of feasibility study becomes necessary because of the sustenance and continuity of the schemes; many of these succor provisions are capital intensive.

For each of the categories identified above there are numerous services associated with it and churches can set up various agencies to cater for the needs in each area.

Humanity Services

The church's humanitarian efforts are aimed at relieving distress of individuals, families, and communities who are victims of one natural disaster or another, irrespective of their religions. Christian churches offer hope and strengthen the self-reliance with belief in the potential for a better life. This includes prison ministry, old age concerns, wheelchair distribution, provision of potable water, provision of relief materials to victims of accidents or other natural disasters, and emergency response (volunteers). Its responsibilities also include charity activities, such as visits to motherless babies' homes and handicapped children's homes with gifts.

The activities of the churches in this area are too numerous to mention. For example, a visit to the website of the SOS Children Villages Nigeria, who are committed to the mission of improving the lives of orphaned and abandoned children in Nigeria, will show you a list of their numerous partners and donors. Sixty per cent of them are churches and agencies within the churches (SOS 2015). The Redeemed Christian Church of God has been involved in the provision of potable water (boreholes) in some rural areas in Lagos State and elsewhere in the country for years. The activities of Deeper Life Bible Church are commendable in providing food, accommodation, and basic toiletries to the poor and needy who are able to make it to the yearly Easter and Christmas and New Year retreats (Ojo 1992: 166). The Pacelli School for the Blind in Lagos is owned by the Catholic Church, Wesley School for the Deaf in Lagos is owned by the Methodist Church, and leper colonies in various parts of the country are owned by the Anglican Communion.

Educational Development

Over the years, churches have been involved in the provision and development of quality education all over the world. In Nigeria the Christian missionaries are credited for introducing and developing formal education. The first mission primary school (the Methodist Mission School) was opened in Badagry in 1843, and forty-six years later (1899) the colonial government built its own first primary school in Lagos (Dzurgba 1991: 186–195). In recent years many Nigerian churches have established secondary schools and universities as a result of low-quality teaching, lack of adequate infrastructure, lack of teachers, students' moral decadence, and the incessant closure of universities and strikes by teachers and lecturers.

The task of educating the children is a joint responsibility of the government and the church (the private owners) (Adebiyi 2001: 40); the government make all educational policies, while owners provide everything to make the policies work to their own advantage (Ositelu 2011).

The immediate past Archbishop, Metropolitan and Primate of All Nigeria, Most Rev. Peter J. Akinola, observes that 'without comprehensive education, we will never fulfil our God-given potential as human beings and as a nation' (Adebiyi 2009: 91). As a result, churches are now school proprietors, employing experienced and qualified teachers and building modern school infrastructure. A number of them are providing boarding accommodation for pupils and generally making the learning environments conducive, improving students' moral standards based on godly principles, and thereby improving the academic standard of the pupils.

Many churches have now gone a step further by founding private universities, which are competing favourably with the federal and state-owned universities in terms of academic content, infrastructure, and human resources. Many of them have been criticized for charging high tuition fees, thereby becoming unaffordable to many families, especially the financially disadvantaged ones. However, considering other factors, especially the cost of living in Nigeria, commensurate fees must be charged so as to maintain and improve the standard already set and take it even further.

Also, many of them are also in the habit of giving scholarships and grants to outstanding pupils, especially those from financially poor backgrounds. The demand for university education in Nigeria is on the increase due to a number of factors. Chief among them are the population explosion and the limited number of spaces available in federal and state-owned universities. Below is a list of some of the private Christian universities and their establishing churches (Omotoye 2015).

- Covenant University, Otta, Ogun state, established by the Living Faith Church
- Babcock University, Ilisan, Remo, Ogun state, established by the Seventh Day Adventist Church
- Bowen University, Iwo, established by the Baptist Church
- Benson Idahosa University, Benin, established by the Church of God Mission
- Bingham University, established by the ECWA Church
- Redeemed University, established by the Redeemed Christian Church of God
- Ajayi Crowther University, Oyo, established by the Anglican Communion
- Crawford University, Igbesa, established by the Apostolic Faith Church
- Caritas University, Abuja, established by the Catholic Church
- Wesley University of Technology, Ondo, established by the Methodist Church

The list is not exhaustive; many churches are still in the process of launching out in the same direction. Generally, education with the mission schools has become an enviable venture for many churches. Perhaps motives differ from one church to the other. The important issue, however, is the fact that the gap created by the inability of the state to provide adequate facilities for a teeming population of children and youth is being filled by the church.

Employment Generation

Many churches in Nigeria have business interests in many corporate organisations outside the church system, and through these companies employment is provided to many in society. For instance, the LoveWorld Ministries (also known as Christ Embassy) is the owner of Moneycom Microfinance Limited, LoveWorld Television Network, LoveWorld Publishing House, LoveWorld Records Limited (all in Lagos, Nigeria) and a host of other business interests. The Diocese of Lagos West, Anglican Communion owns the Multipurpose Conference Centre (City of God) at Ipaja, Lagos, Trinity Gardens Limited, Lagos and a microfinance company. The Synagogue Church of All Nations (SCOAN) owns the Emmanuel Television Network and the SCOAN Hotels.

Many Christian churches are involved in the area of capital developments—the establishment of hospitals, clinics, schools, recreational centres, and vocational centres, and the like. Through these establishments jobs are created and means of economic livelihood are provided. The clerical and secretarial staff handles administrative affairs, and unskilled workers, such as gardeners, security personnel, and drivers, are on the payroll of many churches as employees. Thus, churches are helping to reduce the number of people roaming the streets in search of jobs. According to Afe Adogame, 'to attempt to get the statistics or a precise figure of the employees under all the religious organizations in Nigeria is to attempt to count the stars in the sky'(1999: 22–45).

Churches are springing up every day, and the national bodies, Christians Association of Nigeria (CAN) and Pentecostal Fellowship of Nigeria (PFN), do not have accurate records and data to facilitate a proper statistical research of the number of personnel within the church.

Social and Ethical Development

There are certain values and ethical principles that the church needs to uphold and find outlets for in society, because they are sacrosanct to decent co-existence in society. That was the reason for the Ten Commandments, which are principles for establishing good and healthy relationships in society. This could be done through periodic seminars, public lectures, newsletters, or similar forums devoid of any religious coloration that will bring people of different faiths together. The Bible teaches about other ethical norms which people know instinctively (Romans 1: 26–32; 2: 14–15). This is not about imposing Christian values but what many considered as 'natural law'. These are timeless ethical principles and therefore do not require cultural adaptation, but they are fast fading out, because nobody is passing them on to the younger generation. These principles include respect for other people, especially the elderly, fear of God, and treating all human beings with love and meeting their basic needs. For a better society, the younger generation needs good guidance, moral teachings, and resources with which to produce positive results in the present and later in life, as they are the leaders of tomorrow.

In this regard, the publication of educative, informative, edifying, and character-developing books and other Christian literature would help. Many Nigerian Christian leaders are living up to expectations in this area, as many of them are prolific writers. Christian film productions are now being used for the same purposes—correcting, edifying, and teaching young and old good morals and values that can help both individuals and society. Aside from this, the opportunities presented by media platforms these days to communicate and reach people remotely is also being used by churches to showcase and present the gospel in other dimensions so as to impact society in a positive way. Preaching, teaching, praying, and interview sessions on radio and television stations are some of the avenues that are currently used but can still be explored for further advantages. Also, in this category is Information Communication Technology (ICT). This will help to expand the church's frontiers if fully explored.

Socially, a number of agencies can be created within local churches to respond to the perennial suffering that many people in the society are facing. This should not be limited to members of these churches who find themselves in this category, but it has to be extended to members of the public too.

The establishment of vocational centres in different locations within their various localities is an idea that is worth trying, where students (young and old) are taught diverse skills and crafts that could help alleviate the poverty level in society. If possible, the graduates of the vocational centres could be assisted with loans to take off in their chosen fields. These loans, coupled with various seminars and teachings on 'how to create wealth' by seasoned businessmen and women, will go a long way in reducing unemployment.

There could also be social welfare ministries or agencies within churches, where the privileged and financially well-endowed members could donate money or other resources that could be used in taking care of internal needs of the less privileged, the sick, the aged, and widows within the churches.

Governance by Example

First and foremost, the church needs to put its own house in order. The church authorities, as much as possible, should demonstrate transparency, accountability, equality, inclusiveness, and conformity to the will of God as written in scripture. The more the local churches practice these things, the more they are witnessing to local, state, and national governments on how things ought to be done. Leadership should avoid materialism, extravagant living, and autocratic tendencies. Churches will inevitably become points of reference in their localities and possibly facilitators of change.

On an individual level, the church needs to train its members on how to demonstrate the same qualities expected of the church as a whole so that they can bring these principles to bear on the structures of the society wherever they find themselves.

Improved Economy

It was pointed out in chapter three that there will always be connections one way or another between the church and the state in a secular society. The church needs the state and the state needs the church. The church and the government need to partner in certain areas for the good of their common interests, which are the people and society as a whole.

The church can help improve the economy in a number of ways. In a third-world country like Nigeria, except for those who are employed by the organised private sectors, many civil servants and other government parastatals do not pay taxes. The church can help improve the economy in this regard through enlightening speeches urging members to pay their taxes, as the government cannot do much without the taxes. Although it is their civic responsibility to do so, they still need to be reminded because many do not like to pay. It is only when taxes are paid that the church can rise up to demand on their behalf that certain amenities are needed in certain areas.

The individual churches could motivate their members to become entrepreneurs by providing business education for members and non-members. Each local church could go a step further by granting take-off loans to those willing to start business, and with the assistance rendered by individual members to one another, many businessmen and women could be produced, thereby improving the lots of the people concerned and helping to improve the economy at the same time.

Also, the local churches can encourage individual members work as volunteers in local councils, community development projects, and special events within their localities, which otherwise would cost the local authority huge amounts of money to employ paid personnel. Good examples were the volunteers (mostly youth of the diocese of Lagos West Anglican Communion, church of Nigeria) who participated in the 2007 and 2011 elections in various parts of Lagos state for the Independent National Electoral Commission (INEC) and during local government elections for the Lagos state Independent Electoral Commission (LASIEC). These volunteers are of economic value to the state, because if they have to get people to work instead of the volunteers, they must be paid.

Spiritual and Moral Development

Spiritual activities are not social actions. However, they have social consequences for society in that those who are either converted to Christianity or are convinced about some Christian principles or are generally affected positively through an evangelical activity will probably go back and live a better moral life that will affect their businesses, families, and friends, thereby bringing peaceful co-existence and better interpersonal relationships in the polity.

Anyone who accepts to be a Christian must also be ready to accept the moral encumbrances and consequences that come with it. These are more than individual private moral rules; they include social behaviours and public integrity. Any attempt to describe Christianity devoid of testimonial about its reforming influence on the morality of society is denying the moral dimension to faith. The more people turn to God, the better society we all have. It is expected of Christians to be exemplary in conduct both privately and publicly, and this can only be possible when the ministers or pastors are teaching and preaching the fundamental truth of the gospel all the time.

Healthcare Development

Healthcare is one of the legacies the missionaries left for the mission-established churches in Nigeria, and it is one of the major areas where the church still needs to focus its attention. Governments at various levels in Nigeria have put in so much in terms of funding and providing hospitals, hospital equipment, and the relevant infrastructure to make many state hospitals and health centres ultra-modern, and for this they can be commended. However, despite their efforts, there are still gaps to be filled. Probably because of the human congestion in many states, the government's efforts are inadequate; hence, many of them are seeking help from the private sector and

The Mandates of the Church

from well-meaning individuals to partner with them to help establish hospitals. In Lagos state in particular, the Commissioner for Health used news media to seek private partners, because the state government could do it alone (Adekunle 2009).

The church has to rise to the occasion not exactly as a partner but as the church's duty. The agenda of the missionaries (CMS) to Nigeria was to provide quality education and quality health delivery to society and to plant churches and win souls for the kingdom of God. Not many churches will be able to fund the building and equipping of a standard hospital, but there could be a sort of partnership arrangement within denominations, across denominations, and at the national level, that is, the Christian Association of Nigeria (CAN) or the Pentecostal Fellowship of Nigeria (PFN). Also, agencies or departments could be set up in local churches with the responsibility of organising periodic public lectures on health and the medical concerns of the populace. Special public health publications could be produced with the help of medical personnel who are members of local churches. Evangelical outreaches could be organised, with free medical consultation and treatment of minor ailments in various communities; ailments such as malaria, hypertension, yellow fever and diabetes could be taken care of by this group.

By and large, the church's involvement in many aspects of people's lives in society, particularly the social and political aspects, is part of the cultural mandate of the church. Even though these are areas that are ordinarily meant for the government, the church has to step in to ease the sufferings of the masses with innovative ideas and support the government's efforts.

Chapter Six

The Contribution of the Church to Lagos Society

If you can't do great things, do little things with great love. If you can't do them with great love, do them with a little love. If you can't do them with a little love, do them anyway. Love grows when people serve.

— John Ortberg,
The Me I Want to Be: Becoming God's Best Version of You

This chapter gives a historical overview of Christianity as a religion in Lagos, Nigeria, looking at how it started, how it evolved, and the impact it has had on society up to now.

The Advent of Christianity in Lagos

Lagos came to prominence during the era of the Atlantic slave trade when it became a slaving port. The

The Mandates of the Church

European slave merchants preferred it to other ports along the coast of Niger because of the interaction and understanding between the European Atlantic traders and the indigenous canoe-borne traders along the coastal lagoons. According to George A. Robertson, a British trader, Lagos was a desirable place on the coast for European traders and settlers 'as it lies between the great branches of the Niger and Western trade; the inhabitants are already disposed to habits of industry' (Smith 1979: 19). The Lagos channel and the lagoon were used to approach the hinterland communities, where slaves and cloth were purchased.

After the abolitionists successfully championed the fight against the slave trade, it was abolished by Britain in 1807 (Afigbo 2006: 1), and other European countries at different times promulgated laws banning the same. A preventive squadron of the British Royal Navy was stationed along the coast of West Africa intended to help stop the obnoxious trade (Geiss 1974: 46). Despite these efforts, the trade continued unabated in some areas of West Africa, including Lagos. Consequently, evangelical initiatives arose in order to put a final stop to the trade. A good example was the suggestion by Thomas Fowell Buxton as quoted by Stephen A. Fagbemi in his book, *Who Are the Elect in 1 Peter?* He said:

> We must elevate the minds of her people and call forth the resources of her soil ... Let Missionaries and school masters, the plough and the spade, go together and agriculture flourish; the avenues to legitimate commerce will be opened; confidence between mam and man will be inspired; whilst civilization

> will advance as the natural effect, and Christianity operate as the proximate cause, of this happy change. (2007: 198)

This was like a blueprint for the British government and the missionaries to work on to bring about the much-desired end to the slave trade. With the backing of the anti-slavery movement, the missionaries began an exploratory voyage of the River Niger area to the interior country in 1841 (Oduyoye 1969: 9). According to Fagbemi, 'this expedition exhibited a rare combination of Christianity, Civilization and Commerce (the 3Cs)' (2007: 198). This initial attempt, tagged 'The Bible and the Plough', was not successful for a number of reasons; chief among them was the substantial loss of lives among the white members of the expedition, thereby confirming the belief that West African Coast was the 'White Man's Grave' (Kalu 1978: 19). The other main reason for its failure was the linguistic difficulty of communicating the gospel (Oduyoye 1969: 10). The missionaries learnt an important lesson—that the 'brunt of the penetration of the West African interior must be borne by persons with black skins' (Oduyoye 1969: 10). This development dampened the zeal of the missionaries, the government, and the anti-slavery leaders. However, it did not stop the missionaries from rethinking their strategy (Kalu 1978: 20), and the support provided by the anti-slavery movements eventually paid off (Ajayi 1965: 8–9).

A new and momentous step toward taking the gospel into the hinterland of Nigeria, the Yoruba land in particular, was inspired by converted liberated slaves of Nigerian origin who had settled in Sierra Leone. They were clamouring to return home (Omoyajowo 1995: xi), and those that had returned earlier were also making

'Macedonian call' to the missionaries for help (Oduyoye 1969: 9).

These requests were granted. Many of the emancipated slaves from Sierra Leone returned home, and the church Missionary Society (CMS) sent Henry Townsend as missionary to work with those who had converted. He arrived in Badagry in December 1842 (Omoyajowo 1995: xi). According to Professor Omoyajowo (the former head of the Department of Religious Studies at the University of Ife, now Obafemi Awolowo University), 'The Methodists had a few months earlier sent Thomas B. Freeman their missionary in Gold Coast (Ghana) to visit Badagry and Abeokuta' (Omoyajowo 1995: xi). Based on the reports of these missionaries to their respective organisations, teams of missionaries were sent to join the Christian campaign.

Their activities initially were restricted to Badagry (Lagos state). There they built a church, a school, and the Mission House, which is believed to be the first two-storey building in Nigeria (Oduyoye 1969: 26). Although the first missionary post was established in Badagry, they later moved into the hinterland because of the uncooperative attitude of their host community, who became unhelpful possibly because of their loss of earnings due to the abolition of the slave trade (Nojimu-Yusuf and Osoba 2011). Abeokuta was their next stop. They settled there, along with many of the returning liberated slaves, the majority of who were Christians and missionaries in their own right (Smith 1979: 13).

Overall, missionary work was initially limited to the areas between Lagos and Ibadan. The Church of England's Church Missionary Society (CMS) was the trail blazer (Ludwig et al., 2004: 135), followed by other denominations from Britain, Canada, and the United states, and in the 1860s by Roman Catholic religious orders (ARTSCARE 2011). The CMS was particularly active among the Yoruba, of which Lagos is part, while the Catholic missionaries held sway among the Igbo people.

Therefore, Christianity came to Lagos, Nigeria through Christian missionary endeavours in the nineteenth century. The missionaries came with a resolve to evangelise, convert many indigenes to Christianity, plant churches, and establish legitimate commerce in place of the obnoxious slave trade that had predominated.

The Influence of Christian Missionaries

The influence of the missionaries on society was huge, but it was a mixed blessing, particularly in Lagos. By 1842, both the missionaries and the returning liberated slaves avoided the island of Lagos because it had become a notorious seaport for slave trading, even surpassing Badagry (Oduyoye 1969: 51). Modupe Oduyoye succinctly summarises the situation:

> By 1829 Lagos had overtaken Badagry in importance as the leading slave port; but for same reason it was less likely to attract returning freed slaves, although it lay more directly on the route to Abeokuta. Badagry, which was already losing its slave-trading business to Lagos was preferable; the route from there to Abeokuta was safer, if more difficult, than tracks inland from Lagos. Moreover, the returning slaves were badly treated at – still greatly involved in slave trading – whereas at Badagry they were

welcome by the chief (Wawu) of the Yoruba quarter in the Ahovikoh ward. (1969: 22).

However, penetration into the island of Lagos eventually became possible thanks to the dynastic struggle between Oba Kosoko and Akintoye. The former supported the continuity of the slave trade, while the latter wanted it stopped and replaced with legitimate commerce. This instability and the tussle between these two left the British naval troop with no option but to take control of Lagos by sacking the Oba (King) who supported the slave trade and recognising Akintoye as Oba of Lagos after he was made to sign a treaty pledging to end the slave trade (Oduyoye 1969: 510). Subsequently, the British troop annexed the port of Lagos in 1861 (Law 1983: 21–348).

There is a counter claim that the sacking of Oba Kosoko was not based on his refusal to sign the anti-slavery trade treaty, but was for firing at the British flag that had been fraudulently hoisted to frighten him and his chiefs, who had earlier asked for five days to consider the proposal. According to this account, Kosoko was not really given an opportunity to either accept or reject the proposal. Adekunle Alli writes:

> It must, however, be noted for posterity that John Beecroft, the British Consult, ordered naval attack on King Kosoko, not because he refused to sign the anti-Slave Trade Treaty, but for 'firing on (British) flag of truce' fraudulently hoisted to frighten King Kosoko and his chiefs who had earlier pleaded for five days to consider the proposal. (2002)

His request for five days to consider whether or not to sign the treaty might have been viewed by John Beecroft as another way of saying no—hence the military invasion, his removal, and the later enthronement of his rival Akintoye as Oba. Subsequently, Britain steadily extended its control and influence along the coast. Between the years 1861 and 1885 Britain had annexed the rest of the Yoruba states and the states along the River Niger and Benue (Falola and Heaton 2008: 93).

In Lagos, after the British annexed it, the missionaries were in the forefront of resettling the returning slaves from Sierra Leone, Liberia, Brazil, Cuba, and America. According to G. O. Gbadamosi, Lagos witnessed the establishment and expansion of Christianity with the migration into Lagos and its hinterland of the ex-slaves from Sierra Leone and the New World (1975: 176). The missionaries encouraged many of them to return to their homes and re-unite with their families. According to Omoyajowo, 'between 1839 and 1842 not fewer than 500 freed slaves had returned to their homes' (1995: 17) and re-united with their kith and kin.

Already some of the returning ex-slaves settled in Abeokuta had started to have impact on the society, as many local people were becoming Christians. This led to some problems for some local converts in Abeokuta in 1867 (Ajayi et al., 1998: 81). They were expelled from the community by their kinsmen, but the missionaries (again with the help of the then Governor of Lagos, Governor Glover) settled them at Ebute-Metta in a place known today as Ago Egba (Egba Camp). However, the success of the mission work in the Yoruba parts of the southern Nigeria cannot and should not be credited to the

The Mandates of the Church

European missionaries alone. The returning ex-slaves also had a tremendous impact. Caleb Oladipo writes:

> As early as 1792, Christianity arrived in Africa through many groups of Christians of African birth or descent who had come to faith in Christ as plantation slaves or soldiers in the British army during the American war of independence, or as farmers or as squatters in Nova Scotia after it. They took their own preachers and church leaders to Africa and their churches were functioning before the arrival of modern missionaries from the Western world. Therefore, the making of Christian Africa cannot be exclusively attributed to Western missionaries. The contribution of African influence and Africans' unique interpretation and application of the Gospel have been enduring elements in the making of Christian Africa in the twentieth century. (1996: 325)

This position is corroborated by the account of David Ihenacho. He is also of the opinion that the emancipated slaves were at the forefront of evangelization of their people; missionaries only supported them when they saw them making so much impact (2004: 48).

Meanwhile, other freed slaves and their descendants from Sierra Leone and Liberia (also known as the Saros), with the help of missionaries and collaboration with the Governor of Lagos, were settled in Tinubu Square, Olowogbowo, and Breadfruit areas of the island. The other group of freed slaves from Brazil and Cuba (also known as Agudas) were settled in the Aguda, Bamgbose, and Campus Square areas (Falola and Childs 2004: 356). Many of these returnees had been greatly influenced by Christianity and western culture (Williams 2005: 111). The Agudas were mainly Catholics, while the Saros were mainly Protestants.

The missionaries have been blamed for many woes in Africa, particularly in Nigeria. This is because they were seen as agents of the colonial administration and Christianity was seen as an effective colonial tool for stable rule. Adam Smith was quoted by Apkenpuun Dzurgba as saying that he was persuaded that religion could be used effectively to the advantage of the government to establish itself and to set up stable colonial rule. Hence, the British government supported missions morally, materially, and financially (Dzurgba 1991: 186–195). Though this might be true to some extent, the missionaries and the colonial government had their differences. A very good example was the prohibition of the missionaries from making incursions into certain parts of the northern protectorate. The colonial government restricted the missionaries from penetrating into Northern Nigeria, where Islam was already entrenched, even when Islamic chiefs were sending invitations to the missionaries to come and establish schools and mission stations in their domains (Crampton 1975: 64). The colonial government, through their officers, claimed:

> The exclusion of Christian missionaries from Muslim areas was necessary to avoid the development of religious fanaticism. Colonial officials also claimed that the emirs had never agreed that missionaries should operate in the emirates and added that they would not

want the missionaries to be embarrassed, for the embarrassment of an European was their own embarrassment (Mbachirin 2006: 62).

The reasons for this resistance as enumerated by E. P. T. Crampton (1975: 64) and Matthew Kukah (1993: 7) were selfish and impious. This can be said to be true, judging from Frederick Lord Lugard's protest about the missionaries. He complained, 'The preaching of equality of Europeans and natives, however true from a doctrinal point of view, is apt to be misapplied by people in a low stage of development, and interpreted as an abolition of class distinction' (Boer 1979: 75).

With hindsight, Dzurgba comments, 'The colonial society was never a consensual society. Its authorities had the monopoly of the means of violence. The colonial system of rule was paternalistic, authoritarian, and dictatorial in character and function' (1991: 186–195). The conclusion follows that Christian missionaries were a disruptive force in African society (Mlaponi 2008). To the detriment of the colonised community, they (the colonialists and missionaries) promoted policies of enslavement and exploitation (Smith 1972: 103–132). Mary Kindsley, a British colonial officer, anticipated the grief and indelible marks colonialism would leave upon Africa and Africans. She posits that 'Whatever we do in Africa today, a thousand years hence there will be Africans to thieve or suffer from it' (Nicolson 1969: iv).

Regardless of all the flaws, considering the hostile environments they worked in and the restrictions the colonial government was using to impede their advancement and the development of the people, the missionaries still made positive and significant impacts in several spheres of life of the host communities, providing good examples for the mainstream and Pentecostal churches of how a church can contribute to the development of society. It is true that their coming might have some connotations of self-gratification and heroic martyrdom (Coleman 1971: 92) or an economic undertone as suggested by Nojimu-Yusuf and Osoba (2011). However, this is not to deny in total the theological motivations which partly drove them to engagement, commitment, devotion, and sacrifice (Dzurgba 1991: 186–195).

The Achievements of the Christian Missionaries

In view of the controversy about whether to blame missionaries for the colonial enslavement and exploitation of the people of Lagos in particular and other Nigerians in general, there is a need to do an appraisal of what they were able to do during the period in question.

First, the Christian missionaries need to be credited for introducing and developing formal education. There were informal ways of teaching or educating indigenes in Yoruba land (including Lagos) before the arrival of the missionaries. The first mission primary school was opened in Badagry in 1843 (Methodist Mission School), and forty-six years later (1899), the colonial government built its own first primary school in Lagos (Dzurgba 1991: 186–195). Rev. James Johnson of the Anglican mission argued that the establishment of schools was a major strategy for evangelism, and it helped Christianity to grow as students were taught the Christian faith and many eventually converted to Christianity (Nojimu-Yusuf and Osoba 2011).

Charles S. Johnson (1951: 3), John S. Mbiti (1999), Raphael J. Njoroge (2004), Apkenpuun Dzurgba (1991), and other scholars have criticised formal or western education in an African setting. They claim that formal education created more problems than it solved. Johnson comments, 'One of the problems of formal education grows out of the fact that it has lost touch with family and that education in the school is frequently in conflict with what is imparted in the family' (1951: 3). On the contrary, Rotimi Adewale describes what western education did to the family setting in Nigeria as 'progress and positive' (2005: 137–147), although he also admitted the fact that there may be few negative impacts, which he advised could be minimised if we can retain some aspects of our traditional culture that impact positively on the family (2005: 137–147).

Johnson probably was writing based on the conflict between Western civilization and African cultural values. Initially, there will always be a discontinuity between the school environment and the home environment for a new student. However, if the missionaries had brought on board some of the basic cultural values of the people, perhaps the discontinuity would have been less obvious. Western or formal education would not be seen as an avenue to de-culturalise the people and bend them more towards 'white' or European cultures and value systems (Onwauchi 1972: 243).

Dzurgba, while acknowledging the initiative of the missionaries in introducing formal education, was also quick to point out that it was not aimed at national development but was just a means of producing clerks (1991: 186–195). He admitted that things did change for better when people started demanding more education after receiving the initial minimum education (1991: 186–195). Eventually, the mission schools produced people with new ideas, abilities, and communication skills, such as mechanics, carpenters, technicians, builders, storekeepers, doctors, nurses, dispensers, laboratory technologists, and electricians (Ogundiran 2005: 520).

The approach of the Christian missionaries in establishing schools was a good way of propagating the gospel, empowering the people via literacy and other skills, and preparing them for effective understanding of what was going on around them. On the other hand, it was used to supply and strengthen the colonial structures and systems and possibly ward off competition from native institutions. Lagos today can boast of several Christian missionary schools from different denominations including Methodist, Anglican, Baptist, Pentecostal churches, and many more.

Second, the missionaries also deserve credit for the growth of legitimate business in place of the slave trade (Oyebade 2004: 272). They encouraged legitimate trade among the local people, and export substitution of palm oil instead of slaves attracted European merchants, while liberating slaves and refugees from interior Lagos (Mabogunje 1968: 259). They were indeed like a business pressure group, educating people on the prospect of intermediary trade between Abeokuta and Lagos and similarly informing them of other legitimate produce that could be marketed to the outside world (Oshodi 2011).

Their help in preserving and developing the local languages cannot be over-emphasised. According to E. A. Ayandele, 'By their efforts the main languages of Nigeria have been preserved as lasting legacy to the Ibo, Yoruba, Efik, Nupe and Hausa' (1966: 283). He noted that the idea was not supported by either the indigenes or the colonial administrators. He writes, 'Upon the Christian missions devolved the task of preserving the vernacular against the wishes of their converts and the indifference of the administrators who preferred the English language' (1966: 283). The indigenes later embraced the idea, as people were taught how to read and write. The vernacular literature was encouraged, and some indigenes were employed as interpreters of English language to the local language group. Toyin Falola, Matthew Heaton (2008: 88) and Saheed Aderinto (2010: 14) are some of the scholars that have acknowledged the efforts of the missionaries at improving communication with local communities by learning their languages, leading to writing and developing an understanding of their cultures. This led to the rise of local scholars, who were able to write in both the local dialect and in English. Dictionaries, educational books, and newspapers were produced in local dialects.

The contribution of a local missionary in this regard cannot be forgotten. Bishop Samuel Ajayi Crowther was one of a few liberated ex-slaves who were educated in England and Sierra Leone before returning home in 1864, after he had been consecrated as a bishop. He was responsible for the interpretation of Holy Bible from English to the Yoruba language (Olofinjana 2010: 16).

Another area where the missionaries were trailblazers and excelled was in the production of newspapers (Falola and Aderinto 2010: 14). CMS established and produced the first Nigerian newspaper in Abeokuta, named *Iwe Irohin* (Adejunmobi 2004: 41). It features Christian news, up-coming events, and social and political comments. The newspaper was also an avenue to educate readers on various subjects and topics and provide information, guidance, and explanations on various issues that concern the citizenry. If Christians are commenting publicly in printed newspapers, then they influence society. The DLW followed these examples, and today the diocese and its leadership are not just social and political commentators but active participants in socio-political activities. In the process of the production of newspapers, the missionaries also established printing press, which also served the need of the community, as some indigenes were trained on how to print and other basic skills.

Missions played a major role in the health sector in Lagos and other parts of the country. It is on record that western medicine was formally set up in Nigeria in the 1860s by the Roman Catholic missionaries in Abeokuta, when the Sacred Heart Hospital was established. In the 1870s other missions followed the example of the Catholic missions by establishing various hospitals, health centres, and clinics in Lagos, Calabar, and other parts of the country. Throughout the colonial era, Christian missions were in the forefront of supplying modern healthcare facilities (*Nigeria Health* 2011).

However, A. G. Onokerhoraye observes that many of these hospitals built by the Christian missionaries are concentrated in the rural areas (1982: 16), probably suggesting an ulterior motive. Israel Ademiluyi and Sunday Aluko-Arowolo were more forthcoming. They concluded that it was another strategy by the missionaries to expand Christianity (2009: 104–110). This conclusion was given more credence by the submission of G. O. Onobonoje. He writes, 'The medical centres established by the missionaries were largely concentrated in the rural areas because of the goal of evangelism, which was to get the rural 'pagan' to embrace the new religion' (1975: 167).

The action of the missionaries shows nothing but foresight, because when governments started building hospitals the rural areas were not on their agenda. They concentrated on the urban areas where there was a high concentration of Europeans and government officials (Home 1983: 165–176). So, if the missionaries had not built hospitals, mobile clinics, and community dispensary outposts to treat primary health problems of the people in the rural areas, the government would have neglected them.

The missionaries were not just building hospitals; they were also involved in providing training for nurses and paramedics and sponsoring doctors abroad for advanced training.

The inventiveness of the missionaries also covered social services, as they were associated with the establishment of markets, postal services, water supply, electricity, telephone services, radio stations, rehabilitation centres, and hotels (Odumosu, Olaniyi, and Alonge 2009: 23). According to A. D. Galloway, 'the beginnings of modern social services were made by the missions' (Galloway 1960: 63).

Overall, Lagos benefited more than any other part of the nation from the missionaries' benevolence both socially and in terms of infrastructure. This might be because it was the headquarters of the missionaries' activities, coupled with fact that it had always served as the seat of an expanding British commercial and imperial interest in Nigeria (Adebayo 1987: 308), Lagos grew in importance as the economic, social, commercial, political, administrative, and financial centre of the nation (Abiodun 1997). So, the DLW is now following these paths.

The ultimate aim of the missionaries was spreading the gospel in every way possible so that many would come to faith in Christ, but their creativity and ideas continue to have a lot of impact on society socially, politically, economically, and spiritually. By and large, the activities of the missionaries helped the local people and the returning slaves in particular. The liberated slaves were helped to settle easily back into society, and these repatriates from Sierra Leone, Brazil, Cuba, and Liberia later had great influence on the structures and nature of society, thereby affecting the history of Lagos significantly. The contributions and achievements of the missionaries in Lagos cannot be denied, irrespective of the ugly experiences that people might have had during the colonial era.

Contemporary Lagos and Christian Churches

Nigeria gained independence from Britain in 1960, and Lagos remained the capital of the country even at independence. As a result, Lagos experienced rapid and significant growth economically, politically, and socially. The population of the Federal Capital Territory suddenly snowballed as there was an influx of people into the city of Lagos from various parts of the country and beyond, thus turning Lagos into a greater metropolitan city (United Nations 2004: 57).

Consequently, in 1967 the military government of Nigeria promulgated a decree to restructure Nigeria's federation into twelve states to replace the four regions of the Federal Republic of Nigeria. Lagos State was created on 27 May 1967. Its territory was defined as the municipality of the Lagos, Badagry, Ikeja, Ikorodu, and Epe divisions of the former Western Region of Nigeria (Adebayo 2012: 306). Lagos state was formed by the fusion of two areas, the municipality of Lagos on one hand and the other four divisions on the other (*New Face* 2012). Prior to the creation of the state, the two areas were administered by separate political jurisdictions, the

The Mandates of the Church

former by the Federal Government and the latter by the Western Region Government (Olugbemi 1987: 321–322). As a result, what we now have as a new state is the city of Lagos and its neighbouring settlements to the east and west, and the Federal Government and Western Region Government's direct administrative control over the new state is removed (Olugbemi 1987: 321–322).

However, the creation of Lagos State was a challenge, as the new state inherited all the problems and liabilities associated with the city of Lagos and neighbouring settlements. The overwhelming task now was to build and maintain a focused and efficient administration that would be able to blend the various settlements into a wholesome unity of the modern with the ancient. Moreover, it was the responsibility of the new administration to modernize government services to the public, solve the long-time problems of slums, improve on the inadequate sociocultural infrastructures, and revamp other public facilities on a continuous basis.

As Lagos witnessed a great influx of people, so also the city witnessed the proliferation of Christian churches within the metropolis. Apart from the pioneering denominations planted by the missionaries that were well known in Lagos before (the Anglican, Roman Catholic, Baptist, and Methodist churches), there were also the African Independent churches or African Initiated churches (AICs), which are offshoot of the agitation for African cultural expression in the mission-established churches. This was termed 'Ethiopianism' (Kalu 2008: 24). Notable among them are the Cherubim and Seraphim churches (C&S), the Church of the Lord (Aladura), the Christ Apostolic Church (CAC), the Evangelical Church of Yahweh, and the Celestial Church of Christ

(CCC) (Adogame and Omoyajowo 1998: 90). The recent emergence of the Pentecostal and Charismatic churches in the state is also extensive. A few years ago it was reported that 'there were more than 700 churches registered as members of Pentecostal Fellowship of Nigeria (PFN) in 1991 in Lagos state alone' (Adogame 2011: 139). There are no known public records of the present figure in 2013. In this category are Redeemed Christian Church of God (RCCG), Assemblies of God, Latter Rain Assembly, Deeper Life Bible Church, Church of God Mission, Christ Embassy, Foursquare Gospel Church, Living Faith World Outreach Ministry, Household of God, Daystar Christian Centre, and many others, all having Pentecostal and Charismatic affiliation. Many of these churches have branches across the country, but Lagos State remains the headquarters for many of them.

For various reasons many of these churches and denominations chose Lagos State as their missions' headquarters. Some would rather have their headquarters where the established mission churches have theirs so as not to appear inferior to them (Omoyajowo 1982: 4). It is also probable that part of the attraction could also be the level of development within the state and the possibility of building networks with all the tribes, languages, and classes of people that are well represented in Lagos. Lagos is home to just about every language and faith in Nigeria. However, many of these churches have been criticized by members of the public for not meaningfully contributing to the development of the state or the people, and economic gain has been advanced as the reason for their presence in Lagos State (Nsehe 2013; Baiyewu 2013). None the less, a few are still acknowledged as catalysts of social change within society (Omotoye 2013).

Successive administrations in Lagos State established comprehensive developmental programmes of action that could stand the test of time, so as to build on a solid foundation for rapid future development laid by the founding fathers of the state. The programme includes the division of the state into five administrative divisions, which were further divided into twenty local government areas (LGAs), to make for a viable, robust, responsible, and purposeful administration, to cultivate independent and fairly dependable revenue, and to establish a basis for the pursuit of vigorous socio-economic development programs aimed at improving the life of its citizenry (Olugbemi 1987: 321–322).

The contemporary churches in Lagos in particular and Nigeria as a whole have been involved in several socio-political activities for the benefit of the populace either on the individual level or in conjunction with other governmental or non-governmental agencies as already pointed out in the previous chapters. These churches are taking on the roles of the state in the society to minimize the effect of the non-availability of government presence in their localities or its lack of concern for the citizens. However, not all the churches are involved with socio-political activities. There are a few that are introverted in their disposition to public and social issues. Their indifference could be a doctrinal conviction, a lack of understanding in regards to social involvement, or an effort to appear holier than others who choose be involved. However, it could be argued that some of these churches' involvement is not totally out of concern for society, but rather because of how they stand to benefit from such societal development. Apart from the mainline churches, many of the other 'churches are established by individuals, owned by them and used as factory or wheel of fortune for the utmost benefit of the founder and his or her immediate family at the detriment of the worshippers' (Ezeh 2011: 68). Hence, the motives of individual churches might differ.

Nevertheless, those who are aware of the fact that their mandate is not limited to evangelism and conversion of souls are directly or indirectly involved in the cultural mandate—the socio-political issues of their immediate environment.

Concluding Remarks

As a sequel to my research, within the context of Nigeria and Lagos State in particular, it must be acknowledged that the church has contributed to the social and political milieu in society. However, a lot still needs to be done both internally and externally, as there are yet many challenges it must overcome to make any serious widespread impact in every sphere of people's lives. With so many societal problems, based on several years of trials and errors occasioned by historical, human, and natural factors, there is a need for a basic tactical revision of the way forward on the part of the church if it is to continue to be recognised as an agent of change and make a real difference in the society.

Internally, there is a need for the on-going education of members to help them develop the understanding of faith that links the church to society as an essential component of social change. Communal life is an essential component of Christian doctrine and culture. The same can be said of the Lagos (Yoruba) culture, like every other African culture. It is fundamental that this idea of interconnectedness and the holistic nature of life permeate

The Mandates of the Church

every stratum of the church so that the church will be united in purpose, action, and voice. No member will be detached from society or will view the state as an enemy. Rather, they will be ready to support and participate in the social change, having realised through biblical insight that the call to be 'salt and light' in and to the world is a call to good works that is multi-dimensional, ranging from concern and care for the poor and the less privileged to speaking out on behalf of the oppressed and constructive involvement in socio-political problems in society.

Externally, the leadership of the church needs to get a good grasp of the context in which the politicians are operating so that they will be able to contribute effectively to the discourse on public policy; otherwise they will be incapable and unprepared when the chance presents itself. The point here is that there is a difference between ideal and reality. The ideal as the church believes it should be concerns the desirable possibility and the perfect outlook, while reality is the actual outlook (Taekema 2003: 35–36). There is the need for leaders in each local church to recognise the fact that not all the populace will share their views, beliefs, and holistic approach to issues. Opposition does not necessarily come from people of another faith. Other Christian denominations might see issues differently. In that case, there might be some disagreements while engaging others with contrary views before agreements are eventually reached. It is only when the church leaders are careful enough to see and acknowledge these differences that they will appreciate the contexts in which politicians operate. As a result, their political dialogue will be based on awareness of the real world.

In conclusion, the church is playing practical roles in the re-building, recovery, and re-positioning of Lagos state, using various means to accomplish these daunting tasks with limited internally generated resources. The transformation of humanity and reconstruction of a broken society cannot be sorted out by Christian churches remaining detached from politics or refusing to partake in the policy-making process. Social, political, and economic transformations can only be realized through positive Christian involvement in the policy-making process at all levels. The Christian churches have both the biblical mandate and mission to be involved in social justice. There may be opposition from within and without for the sake of its position on societal ills, social actions, and advocacy for social reforms (parts of the holistic mission of the church), but the church must not give up. It must be salt and light within the troubled state and nation. Although the road may be rough, with prayer, exemplary life style, good leadership, consistency, boldness, and honesty, the government, the political elite, the Christian community, and the general public will soon realize what an agent of change the church is.

The church as a stakeholder in society has shown that each local church can contribute in various ways to the development of the state and nation. This demands that the church supports and collaborates with state and local governments where necessary, while at the same time strongly identifying with the underprivileged and the marginalized people in society. It has proven that it is not enough to provide social services that are simply intended to ameliorate the conditions of the ordinary citizen; the church should rather engage in social reformation that will restore hope and dignity to the common man by holding state and local government officials accountable to fundamental standards of good governance.

The challenge before the church, however, is how to keep up the standard it has set for itself as an agent of social and political change in society. The church must open itself to change from within as it transforms itself into an institution in society. It must maintain and sustain its core Christian values by mobilising its constituency for more robust commitment to its goals, helping them to develop Christianity in a way that impacts society—that is, while acknowledging its role in society, it is not excessively and unnecessarily attached to the state or the political elite.

The church cannot just be socially involved and not be politically involved too. After all, in democratic societies there is an axiom from Edmund Burke that 'all that is necessary for the triumph of evil is for good men to do nothing' (Haugen 2002: 67). The message that will be sent out if the church hands off is that of an interest group that has lost hope of making a meaningful difference to society and has nothing to offer beyond its constituency.

Bibliography

Books

Abiodun, J. O., 'The challenges of growth and development in metropolitan Lagos' in Rakodi Carole (ed.), *The Urban Challenge in Africa: Growth and Management of its Large Cities (Mega-city)* (New York, NY: United Nation University Press, 1997).

Abu-Shakrah, Jah, Margaret L. Andersen, and Howard F. Taylor, *Study Guide for Andersen and Taylor's Sociology, Understanding a Diverse Society*, Fourth Edition (Belmont, CA: Wadsworth Publishing Company, 2005).

Ade Ajayi, J. F., *Christian Missions in Nigeria, 1841-1891: The Making of a New Elite* (Essex, UK: Longman Publishing, 1965).

Adebayo, A. G., 'The Controversy over the Choice and Position of a Federal Capital' in Adefuye (ed), *The History of Peoples of Lagos State* (Ikeja, Nigeria: Lantern Books, 1987).

Adejunmobi, Moradewun, *Vernacular Palaver: Imaginations of Local and Non-native Languages in West Africa* (UK: Multilingual Matter Ltd, 2004).

Adelegan, Femi, *Governance: An Insider's Reflections* (Bloomington, IN: AuthorHouse, 2012).

Adepoju, Aderanti, A. L. van Naerssen, and E. B. Zoomers (eds.), *International Migration and National Development in Sub-Saharan Africa* (Leiden, Netherlands: Koninklijke Brill NV, 2008).

Adewuji, Tunji, *Street-Begging in Nigeria* (Ibadan, Nigeria: Spectrum Books Limited, 2007).

Adogame, Afe, and Akin Omoyajowo, 'Anglicanism and the Aladura Churches in Nigeria' in Andrew Wingate (ed.), *Anglicanism: A Global Communion* (New York, NY: Church Publishing Inc., 1998).

Adogame, Afe (ed.), *Who is afraid of the Holy Ghost? Pentecostalism and Globalization in Africa and Beyond* (Trenton, NJ: Africa World Press, 2011).

Afigbo, Adiele Eberechukwu, *The Abolition of Slave Trade in Southeastern Nigeria 1885-1950* (New York, NY: University of Rochester Press, 2006).

Ajayi, E. A., R. O. Ajetunmobi, and S. A. Akindele, A History of the Awori of Lagos State (Lagos, Nigeria: Adeniran Ogunsanya College of Education, 1998).

Alexis, Jonas E., *Christianity's Dangerous Idea, Volume 1* (Bloomington, IN: AuthorHouse, 2010).

Andersen, Margaret L., and Howard Francis Taylor, *Sociology With Infotrac: Understanding a Diverse Society*, 4th Edition (Belmont, CA: Wadsworth Publishing Company, 2007).

Andersen, Margaret L., and Howard Francis Taylor, *Sociology: The Essentials* (Belmont, CA: Wadsworth Publishing Company, 2012).

Arjomand, Saïd Ami, *The Political dimension of Religion* (Albany, NY: State University of New York, 1993).

Ayandele, E. A., *The Missionary Impact on Modern Nigeria 1842-1914, A Political and Social Analysis* (London: Longman, Green and Co. Ltd, 1966).

Bevans, Stephen B., and Roger P. Schroeder, *Constants in Context: A Theology of Mission for Today* (Maryknoll, NY: Orbit Books, 2004).

Bezanson, Randall P., *How Free Can Religion Be?* (Chicago, IL: University of Illinois Press).

Bhowmick, P. K., and Swapan Kumar Pramanick, *Explorations in Anthropology: P. K. Bhowmick and His Collaborative Research Works* (New Delhi: Serials Publications, 2007).

Bill, Simon, Robert L. McDowell, and William, L. Simon, *In search of Business Value: Insuring a Return on Your Technology Investment* (New York, NY: SelectBooks Inc., 2004).

Bilton, Tony, *Introduction to Sociology* (London: Macmillan Publishers, 1981).

Blundo, Giorgio, and Pierre-Yves Le Meur, *The Governance of Daily Life in Africa: Public and Collective Services and their Users* (Leidan, Netherlands: Brill Publishers, 2008).

Boer, Jan Harm, *Missionary Messengers of Liberation*, (A doctoral thesis, Vrije Universiteit, Amsterdam: Rodopi, 1979).

Boer, Roland, *Rescuing the Bible* (Malden, MA: Blackwell Publishing, 2007).

Borg, Marcus, *Conflict, Holiness and Politics in the Teaching of Jesus* (New York, NY: Continuum International Publishing Group, 1984).

Boris, Elizabeth T., C. and Eugene Steuerle (eds.), *Nonprofits & Government: Collaboration & Conflict* (Washington DC: Urban Institute Press, 2006).

Braaten, C. E., *Mother Church: Ecclesiology and Ecumenism*, (Minneapolis, MN: Augsburg Fortress Press, 1998).

Bretherton, Luke, *Christianity and Contemporary Politics: The Conditions and Possibilities of Faith Witness* (Malden, MA: John Wiley & Sons, 2011).

Brockhaus, Maria, *Potentials and Obstacles in the Arena of Conflict and Natural Resource Management* (Gottingen: Cuvillier Verlag, 2005).

Buckser, Andrew, *Communities of Faith: Sectarianism, Identity, and Social Change on a Danish Island* (Oxford: Berghahn Books, 1996).

Burdette, Dallas, *Biblical Preaching and Teaching, Vol.3* (Longwood, FL: Xulon Press, 2010).

Carter, Stephen, *God's Name in Vain: The Wrongs and Rights of Religion in Politics* (New York, NY: Basic Books, 2000).

Chan, Francis, *Crazy Love,* (Colorado Spring: David C. Cook, 2008).

Coleman, James S., *Nigeria: Background to Nationalism* (Berkeley, CA: University of California Press, 1971).

Crampton, E. P. T., *Christianity in Northern Nigeria* (Zaria: Gaskiya Corporation Ltd, 1975).

Cray, Graham, *Mission-Shaped Church* (London: Church Publishing House, 2004).

Culpepper, Raymond F., *The Great Commission: The Solution… (Bible Guide)* (Cleveland, TN: Pathway Press, 2009).

Dawkin, Richard, *The God Delusion* (London: Bantam Press, 2006).

Dukor, Maduabuchi F., *Philosophy and Politics: Discourse on Values, Politics, and Power in Africa* (Lagos: Malthouse Press, 2003).

Durkheim, Émile, Carol Cosman, and Mark Sydney Cladis, *The Elementary Forms of Religious Life - Part 2* (Oxford: Oxford University Press, 2001).

Ebaugh, Helen Rose Fuchs, *Handbook of Religion and Social Institutions* (New York, NY: Springer, 2006).

Eberle, Edward J., *Church and State in Western Society: Established Church, Cooperation and Separation* (Surrey, England: Ashgate Publishing Limited, 2011).

Edmonds, Ennis Barrington, *Rastafari : From Outcasts to Culture Bearers* (Oxford: Oxford University Press, 2002).

Efird, James M., *Marriage and Divorce: What The Bible Says* (Eugene, OR: Wipf and Stock Publishers, 2001).

Efird, James M., *The New Testament Writings: History, Literature, and Interpretation* (Westminster: John Knox Press, 1980).

Eller, Jack David Eller, *Introducing Anthropology of Religion: Culture to the Ultimate* (New York, NY: Routledge, 2007).

Emerson, Michael O., and Christian Smith, *Divided by Faith: Evangelical Religion and the Problem of Race in America* (Oxford: Oxford University Press, 2000).

Enns, Paul, *The Moody Handbook of Theology* (Chicago, IL: Moody Publishers, 2008).

Ezeh, Emeka Jonathan, *Secrets for Endless Wealth* (Milton Keynes, UK: AuthorHouse UK Ltd, 2011).

Fagbemi, Stephen Ayodeji, *Who are the Elect in 1 Peter? A Study in Biblical Exegesis and Its Application to the Anglican Church of Nigeria* (New York, NY: Peter Lang Publishing, Inc., 2007).

Fahlbusch, Erwin, *The Encyclopedia of Christianity, Volume 5* (Grand Rapids, MI: William B Eerdmans Publishing Co, 2008).

Falola, Toyin, and Matt D. Childs, *The Yoruba Diaspora in the Atlantic World* (Bloomington, IN: Indiana University Press, 2004).

Falola, Toyin, and Matthew M. Heaton, *History of Nigeria* (Cambridge: Cambridge University Press, 2008).

Falola, Toyin, and Saheed Aderinto, *Nigeria, Nationalism and Writing History* (Rochester, NY: University of Rochester Press, 2010).

Falola, Toyin, *The Foundations of Nigeria: Essays in Honor of Toyin Falola* (Trenton, NJ: Africa World Press, Inc., 2003).

Falola, Toyin, *Violence in Nigeria: The Crisis of Religious Politics and Secular Ideologies* (Rochester, NY: University of Rochester Press, 2001).

Ferrante, Joan, *Sociology: A Global Perspective, Enhanced* (Belmont, CA: Wadsworth Publishing Company, 2010).

Fowler, Robert Booth, *Religion and Politics in America* (Boulder, CO: Westview Press, 2010).

France, R. T., *The Gospel of Matthew: The New International Commentary of the New Testament* (Grand Rapids, MI: Wm. B. Eerdmans Publishing Company, 2007).

Friedli, Richard, Jan A Jongeneel, Klaus Koschorke, Theo Sundermeier, and Werner Ustoft (eds.), *Intercultural Perceptions and Prospects of World Christianity* (Frankfurt: Peter Lang GmbH, 2010).

Galloway, A. D., 'Missionary Impact on Nigeria,' *Nigeria Magazine*, October, 1960.

Gbadamosi, G. O., 'Patterns and Development in Lagos State Religious History' in Aderibigbe (ed.),

Lagos: *The Development of an African City* (Nigeria: Longman Publishers, 1975).

Geiss, Imanuel, *The Pan-African Movement: A History of Pan-Africanism in America, Europe and Africa* (New York, NY: Africana Publishing Company, 1974)

Gibbs, Eddie, and R. K. Bolger, *Emerging Churches: Creating Christian Community in Postmodern Culture* (London: SPCK, 2006).

Giles, Kevin N., *What on Earth is the Church?* (Downers Grove, IL: Intervarsity Press, 1995).

Goheen, Michael W., and Craig G. Bartholomew, *Living at the Crossroads* (Grand Rapids, MI: Baker Academies, 2008).

Goheen, Michael W., *A Light to the Nations: The Missional Church and the Biblical Story* (Grand Rapids, MI: Baker Academic, 2011).

Hamilton, Peter (ed.), *Emile Durkheim: Critical Assessment* (New York, NY: Routledge, 1990).

Haugen, Gary A., *Good News about Injustice: A Witness of Courage in a Hurting World* (Downers Grove, IL: Intervarsity Press, 2002).

Hofrenning, Daniel J. B., *In Washington but Not of It: The Prophetic Politics of Religious Lobbyists* (Philadelphia, PA: Temple University Press, 1995).

Hornby et al., *Oxford Advanced Learner's Dictionary of Current English* (Oxford: Oxford University Press, 2005).

Hughes, Dewi Arwel, and Matthew Bannett, *God of the Poor* (Carlisle: OM Publishing, 1998).

Hunsberger, George Raymond, and Craig Van Gelder, *The Church Between Gospel and Culture: The Emerging Mission in North America* ((Grand Rapids, MI: Wm. B. Eerdmans Publications, 1996).

Ihenacho, D. O., *African Christianity Rises Volume One: A Critical Study of the Catholicism of the Igbo People of Nigeria* (Bloomington, IN: iUniverse.com, 2004.).

Ireland, R., *Kingdoms Come: Religion and Politics in Brazil* (Pittsburgh, PA: The University of Pittsburgh Press, 1991).

Jersild, P. T., *Spirit Ethics: Scripture and the Moral Life—* (Minneapolis, MN: Augsburg Fortress, 2000).

Johnson, Charles S., *Education and Cultural Crisis* (New York, NY: Macmillan Co., 1951).

Johnstone, Ronald L., *Religion and Society in Interaction: The Sociology of Religion* (Boston, MA: Prentice-Hall Publishers, 1975).

Jones, Stephen P., *Criminology* (London: LexisNexis Publisher, 2001).

Jong, Paul C., *What God is Saying to Us Through the Epistle to the Ephesians* (Seoul, Korea: Hephzibah Publishing House, 2008).

Joo-Cheong, Tham, *Money and Politics: The Democracy We Can't Afford* (Sydney, Australia: University of New South Wales Press Ltd, 2010).

Kalu, Ogbu, *African Pentacostalism: An Introduction* (New York, NY: Oxford University Press, 2008).

Kalu, Ogbu, *Christianity in West Africa, The Nigerian Story* (Ibadan, Nigeria: Daystar Press, 1978).

Katongole, Emmanuel, *The Sacrifice of Africa: A Political Theology for Africa* (Grand Rapids, MI: Wm. B. Eerdmans Publications, 2010).

Khan, L. Ali, *Theory of Universal Democracy: Beyond the End of History* (The Hague, Netherland: Martinus Nijhoff Publishers, 2003).

Komblum, William, *Sociology in a Changing World* (Belmont, CA: Wadsworth, Cengage Learning, 2011).

Kukah, Matthew H., *Religion, Politics and Power in Northern Nigeria* (Ibadan, Nigeria: Spectrum Books, 1993).

Lasisi, Hairi, *Destiny 2 Destiny* (Bloomington, IN: iUniverse, 2012).

Lewis, Jonathan (ed.), *World Mission: An Analysis of the World Christian Movement Part 1: The Biblical Historical Foundation: 001* (Pasadena, CA: William Carey Library Pub; second edition, 1994).

Lloyds-Jones, D. M., *Studies in the Sermon on the Mount Vol. 1* (Grand Rapids, MI: Wm. B. Eerdmans Publishing Company, 1991).

Ludwig, Frieder, Afeosemime Unuose Adogame, Ulrich Berner, and Christoph Bochinger, *European Traditions in the Study of Religion in Africa* (Wiesbaden, Germany: Otto Harrassowitz KG, 2004).

Mabogunje, Akin, *Urbanisation in Nigeria* (London: Longman, 1968).

Macionis, John J., and Linda M. Gerber, *Sociology 7th Canadian Ed.* (Canada: Pearson Canada Inc., 2010).

Mbachirin, Abraham T., *The Responses of the Church in Nigeria to Socio-Economic, Political and Religious Problem in Nigeria: A Case Study of the Christian Association of Nigeria (CAN)*, PhD Dissertation (Waco, Texas: Baylor University, 2006).

McGuire, Meredith B., *Religion: The Social Context* (Belmont, CA: Wadsworth Thomson Learning Publishing, 2002).

McWhirter, Darien Auburn, *The Separation of Church and State* (Santa Barbara, CA: Greenwood Publishing Group, 1994).

Mercer, Joyce Ann, *Welcoming Children: A Practical Theology of Childhood* (Danvers, MA: Chalice Press, 2005).

Metzge, Paul L., *The Gospel of John: When Love Comes to Town* (Downers Grove, IL: InterVarsity Press, 2010).

Mody, Piloo, *Democracy Means Bread and Freedom* (New Delhi: Abhinav Publications, 2003).

Newbigin, Leslie, *Foolishness to Greek: The Gospel and Western Culture* (Grand Rapids, MI: Wm. B. Eerdmans Publishing Company, 1986).

Newbigin, Leslie, *The Gospel in a Pluralist Society* (Grand Rapids, MI: Wm. B. Eerdmans Publishing Company, 1989).

Nicolson, I. F., *The Administration of Nigeria 1900 to 1960: Men, Methods, and Myths* (Oxford: University Press, 1969).

Nnoli, Okwudiba, *Ethnic Politics in Nigeria* (Enugu, Nigeria: Fourth Dimension Publishing Co. Ltd, 1978).

Norgren, Jill and Serena Nanda, *American Cultural Pluralism And Law* (Westport, CT: Praeger Publishers, 2006).

Odumosu, Olaniyi and Alonge, *Mapping the Activities of Faith-based Organisations in Development in Nigeria* (Birmingham: University of Birmingham, 2009)

Odumuyiwa, E. Ade, "Christianity, Governance and Development: A case Study of Nigeria in the 21stCentury" in *Religion, Governance and Development in the 21st century*. R. A. Raji (ed.) et al.,(2013).

Oduyoye, Modupe, *The Planting of Christianity in Yorubaland 1842-1888* (Ibadan, Nigeria: Daystar Press, 1969).

Ogundiran, Akinwunmi, *Precolonial Nigeria: Essays in Honor of Toyin Falola,* (Trenton, NJ: Africa World Press, 2005).

Ogundiran, Oyebade (ed.), *The Foundations of Nigeria: Essays in Honor of Toyin Falola* (Trenton, NJ: Africa World Press, 2004).

Ojo, Matthew A., 'Deeper Life Bible Church of Nigeria' in Paul Gifford (ed.), *New Dimension in African Christianity* (All Africa Conference of Churches 1992).

Oladipo, C. O., *The Development of the Doctrine of the Holy Spirit in the Yoruba (African) Indigenous Christian Movement* (Oxford: Peter Lang Publishing, 1996).

Olofinjana, Israel, *Reverse in Ministry and Mission: African in the Dark Continent of Europe* (Milton Keynes, UK: AuthorHouse UK Ltd, 2010).

Olugbemi, S. O., 'The Administration of Lagos State 1967–1979', in Adefuye (ed), *The History of Peoples of Lagos State* (Ikeja, Nigeria: Lantern Books, 1987).

Omoyajowo, J. Akinyele, *Cherubim and Seraphim: The History of an African Independent Church* (New York, NY: NOK Publishers International, 1982).

Omoyajowo, *Makers of the Church in Nigeria 1842-1947* (Lagos, Nigeria: CSS Bookshop Ltd. Publishing Unit, 1995).

Onibonoje, G. O., *Africa in the Modern World, The Last One Hundred Years* (Ibadan, Nigeria: Onibonoje Press, 1975).

Onokerhoraye, A. G., *Public Services in Nigeria Urban Areas: A Case Study of Ilorin* (Ibadan, Nigeria:

Nigerian Institute of Social and Economic Research (NISER), 1982).

Osmer, Richard R., *Practical Theology: An Introduction* (Grand Rapids, MI: Wm. B. Eerdmans Publications, 2008).

O'Toole, Roger, *Religion: Classic Sociological Approaches* (Toronto: McGraw-Hill Ryerson Publisher, 1984).

Pearcey, Nancy, *Total Truth: Liberating Christianity from its Cultural Captivity* (Wheaton, IL: Crossway, 2008).

Pilgrim, Walter E., *Uneasy Neighbors: Church and State in the New Testament*, (Minneapolis, MN: Augsburg Fortress Press, 1999).

Pink, Arthur W., *An Exposition of the Sermon on the Mount* (Grand Rapids, MI: Baker Book House, 1953).

Roberts, Keith A., and David Yamane, *Religion in Sociological Perspective* (London: Pine Forge Press, 2011).

Roche, Douglas J., *Bread Not Bombs: A Political Agenda for Social Justice* (Alberta, Canada: The University of Alberta Press, 1999).

Scott, Susie, *Making Sense of Everyday Life* (Cambridge: Polity Press, 2009).

Sharma, Arvind, *The World's Religions after September 11* (Westport, CT: Praeger Publishers, 2009).

Shenk, David W., and Ervin R. Sturtzman, *Creating Community of the Kingdom* (Scottdale, PA: Herald Press, 1988).

Sider, Ronald J., *Evangelism and Social Action: Uniting the Church to Heal a Lost and Broken World* (Grand Rapids, MI: Zondervan Publishing House, 1993).

Simpkins, Robert A., and Behnaz S. Paknejad, *The Global Crosswinds of Change* (Bloomington, IN: Xlibris Corporation Publishing, 2009).

Smith, Christian, *Christian America? What Evangelicals Really Want* (California, CA: University of California Press, 2002).

Smith, E. H., *Nigerian Harvest*, (Grand Rapids, MI: Baker Book House, 1972).

Smith, Robert Sydney, *The Lagos Consulate, 1851-1861* (California, CA: University of California Press, 1979).

Stott, John R. W., *Christian Mission in the Modern World* (Downers Grove, IL: InterVarsity Press, 2008).

Swart, I., *The Church and the Development Debate* (Bloemfontein, SA: African Sun Press, 2006).

Swedberg, Richard, and Ola Agevall, *The Max Weber Dictionary: Key Words and Central Concepts* (California, CA: Stanford University Press, 2005).

Taekema, Sanne, *The Concept of Ideals in Legal Theory* (Hague, Netherlands: Kluwer Law International, 2003).

Taliaferro, Charles, and J. Paul Griffiths, *Philosophy of Religion: An Anthology* (Oxford, UK: Wiley-Blackwell Publishing Limited, 2003).

The Bombay Saint Paul Society, *Positive Attitude for Life* (Bandra, Mumbai: St Paul Press, 2007).

Thiele, Leslie Paul, *Friedrich Nietzsche and Politics of the Soul: A Study of Heroic Individualism* (Princeton, NJ: Princeton University Press, 1992).

ThirdWay Magazine, Vol. 3, No. 6, June 1979, London, Hymns Ancient & Modern Ltd.

Thompson, Ian, *Sociology in Focus: Religion* (London: Longman Group Limited, 1986).

Trompf, G. W., *Cargo Cults and Millenarian Movements: Transoceanic Comparisons of New Religious Movements* (Berlin: Walter de Gruyter, 1990).

United Nation Human Settlements Programme, *The State of the World Cities, 2004/2005: Globalization and Urban Culture,* (London: Earthscan, 2004).

Vakunta, Peter W., *Cry My Beloved Africa: Essays on the Postcolonial Aura in Africa* (Cameroon: Lagga RPCIG, 2008).

Vanhoozer, Kevin J., Craig G. Bartholomew, and Daniel J. Treier, *Dictionary for Theological Interpretation of the Bible* (Grand Rapids, MI: Baker Book House, 2005).

Wagner, Peter C.,'On the Cutting Edge of Mission Strategies' in Winter, R. D., and S. C. Hawthorne (eds.), *Perspective on the World Christian Movement* (Pasadena, CA: Williams Carey Library, 1999).

Weber, Mark (translated by Talcott Parsons), *Protestant Ethic and the Spirit of Capitalism* (Mineola, NY: Courier Dover Publications, 2003).

Weber, Max, *Economy and Society: An Outline of Interpretive Sociology, Volume 1* (California, CA: University of California, 1978).

Weiss, Susan M., and Netty C. Gross-Horowitz, *Marriage and Divorce in the Jewish State: Israel's Civil War* (Lebanon, NH; University Press of New England, 2013).

Wicks, R. J., *Handbook of Spirituality for Ministers* (Mahwah, NJ: Paulist Press, 2000).

Williams, John Rodman Williams, *Renewal Theology: Systematic Theology from a Charismatic Perspective* (Grand Rapids, MI: Zondervan, 2007).

Williams, Lizzie, *Nigeria: The Bradt Travel Guide* (Bucks: UK, Bradt Travels Guide Ltd, 2005).

Williams, Rodman, *Renewal Theology: Systematic Theology from a Charismatic Perspective* (Grand Rapids, MI: Zondervan, 1996).

Williams, Rowan, *On Christian Theology* (UK: Blackwell, 2000).

Woodstock Theological Centre, *The Ethics of Lobbying: Organised Interest, Political Power and the Common Good* (Washington, DC: Georgetown University Press, 2002).

Yu, Xuanmeng (ed.), *Economic Ethics and Chinese Culture, Vol. III.14* (Washington, DC: The Council for Research in Value and Philosophy, 1997).

Articles

Adebiyi, Peter A. The Presidential Address Delivered to the First Session of the Fourth Synod of Diocese of Lagos West on 14 May 2009.

Adebiyi, Peter A., The Presidential Address Delivered to the Second Session of the First Synod of Diocese of Lagos West on 17 May 2001.

Ademiluyi, I. A., and S. O. Aluko-Arowolo, 'Infrastructural Distribution of Healthcare Services in Nigeria: An Overview', *Journal of Geography and Regional Planning*, Vol. 2(5), Olabisi Onabanjo University, Ago Iwoye, Nigeria (May, 2009).

Adewale, Rotimi, 'Paradox of "Progress": The Role of Western Education in the Transformation of the Family in Nigeria', *Anthropologist Journal*, 7(2), Obafemi Awolowo University, Ile-Ife, Nigeria (2005).

Adogame, Afe, 'Religion and Economic Development in Nigeria', *The Nigerian Journal of Economic History*, Vol. 2 (1999): pp. 22–45.

Dzurgba, A., 'A History of Christian Missions in Nigeria: A Developmental Approach', *Asia Journal of Theology*, Vol. 5, No. 1, NEAAST & BTESSC, Singapore (April,1991), pp. 186–195.

Home, R. K., 'Town Planning, Segregation and Indirect Rule in Colonial Nigeria', *Third World Planning Review*, Vol.5 (2) (1983), pp. 165-176.

Law, Robin, 'Trade and Politics behind the Slave Coast: The Lagoon Traffic and the Rise of Lagos, 1500–1800', *Journal of African History*, Vol.24 (1983), pp. 321-348.

Odozor, Paulinus I., 'God, Nigeria, and the Church: A Theological Essay on the Church and Politics in Nigeria', *Encounter: Journal of African Life and Religion* (Rome), Vol. 8 (2008), pp. 40–58.

Onwauchi, P. C., 'African Peoples and Western Education', *The Journal of Western Education*, Vol.41, No.3 (Summer, 1972), p. 243.

Walls, Andrew, 'Structural Problems in Mission Studies', *International Bulletin of Missionary Research*, Vol. 15, No.4 (October, 1991), pp. 146–155.

Online Sources

<http://saharareporters.com/interview/punch-interview-lets-tax-big-business-churches%E2%80%94falana> [Accessed on 14/04/13].

<http://www.soskdiafme.org/Nigeria/partners/other_sponsors.php> [Accessed on 20/02/2015].

Adekunle, Aliyu, 'Commissioner Seeks Private Partnership in Health Sector', *Vanguard Newspaper*, Nigeria, 19th

March, 2009. Also available on: http://allafrica.com/stories/200903190317.html [Accessed on 14/07/11].

Alli, Adekunle, 'Lagos from the Earliest Times to British Occupation: Transitional Regime' (2002) <http://cefolassaocoed.net/index.php?option=com content&view=article&id=61&Itemid=69&limitstart=5> [Accessed on 21/03/11].

Aro, Olaide, 'Towards the People's Constitution in Nigeria' <http://www.academia.edu/879199/TOWARDS_THE_PEOPLES_CONSTITUTION_IN_NIGERIA> [Accessed on 06/02/13].

ARTSCARE: <http://www.beadmuseumaz.org/yoruba/yoruba.chapter.2.b.asp>, [Accessed on 29/04/11].

Baiyewu, Leke, *Lets Tax Big Business churches*,

Birzulis, Philip, 'Baltic People Remember Their Joint Struggle for Independence' <http://www.baltictimes.com/news/articles/23392/> [Accessed on 12/03/13].

Deb DeRosso, 'The Structural Functional Theoretical Approach', (2003). <http://www.wisc-online.com/Objects/ViewObject.aspx?ID=I2S3404> [Accessed on 11/03/13].

Eastern Europe and the Commonwealth of Independent states 1999, 4th Edition (London: Europa Publications Ltd, 1999) [Accessed 30/12/10].

Fraser, Sean, 'Norway Abolishes State-Sponsored Church of Norway' <http://digitaljournal.com/article/324906> [Accessed on 29/01/13].

Harris, J., The Independent, Obituary: The Rev. Donald English, 31/08/98, <http://www.independent.

co.uk/arts-entertainment /obituary-the-rev- donald-english-1175193.html>

Ike, Obiora,,The Church and Civil Society: The Case of Nigeria' <www.kas.de/db files/.../7 dokument dok pdf 9863 2.pdf> [Accessed on 25/02/13].

Kalu, Ogbu U., 'Faith and Politics in African: Emergent Political Theology of Engagement in Nigeria' <www.calvin.edu/ henry/archives/lectures/ kalu.pdf.> [Accessed on 25/02/13].

Kerr, Glenn, 'Ekklesia: Its form and function' <http://www. hallmarkbaptist.com/ekklesia. htm> [Accessed on 27/05/11].

Krell, Keith, 'Mission Possible' <https://bible. org/seriespage/ 2-mission-possible- matthew-513-16> [Accessed: 31/01/15].

Lagos State Government <http://www. lagosstateonline.com/ govhistory.php?node=2> [Accessed on 30/01/12].

Mlaponi, Frederick, 'Colonialism in Africa' (June, 2008) <http://www.novelguide. com/a/ discover/aes 01/ aes 01 00093. html> [Accessed on 16/03/11].

The New Face of Lagos <http://newfaceoflagos.com/mobolajijohnson.html>[Accessed on 30/01/12].

'NGO's Non-Profit and Humanitarian Activities in the Nigeria Water Industry' <http://www.hydratelife.org/?p=1892> [Accessed on 20/02/2015].

Nigeria History of Modern Medical Services, <www.nigerianbestforum.com/index.php?topic=55451.0> [Accessed on 18/03/11].

Nojimu-Yusuf and Osoba, 'The Growth and the Development of Christianity in Lagos State' <http:// cefolassaocoed.net /index.php?option=com

content&view=article&id=77& Itemid=83> [Accessed on 15/03/11].

Nsehe, Mfonobong, 'The Five Richest Pastors in Nigeria' <http://www.forbes. com/sites/mfonobongnsehe/2011/06/07/the-five-richest -pastors-in-nigeria/> [Accessed on 14/04/13].

Omotoye, Rotimi Williams, 'A Critical Examination of the Activities of Pentecostal Churches in National Development in Nigeria. <http://www. cesnur. org/2010/ omotoye.htm> [Accessed on 14/04/13].

Oshodi Family, 'Who Are the Real Lagosians?' <www.oshodi.org/ history/lagosians. html> [Accessed on 1/02/2011].

Ositelu, Ayo, 'BMJS: Continuing a Tradition of Excellence', *Guardian* Newspaper, Nigeria, 5th August, 2011, available at <http://odili.net/ news/source/2011/aug/5/20. html> [Accessed on 23/05/12].

Roxborogh, John, 'Missiology after Mission?' <http://roxborogh.com/missiology.htm> [Accessed on 25/02/13].

Sociological Theories of Religion <http://www.cliffsnotes.com/study guide/Sociological -Theories-of-Religion.topicArticleId-26957, articleId-26931.html> [Accessed on 11/03/13].

The Division of Labor in Society (1893) <http://durkheim.uchicago. edu/Summaries/dl.html> [Accessed on 11/03/13]

The Observatory, Dec.2010, 'Shadow Report on Intolerance and Discrimination against Christians in Europe', Vienna, ISBN: 978-3-9503055-1-7, <http://www.intoleranceagainstchristians.eu/fileadmin/user_upload/FiveYear_Report_Intolerance

against Christians_in_Europe_-_online_ version. pdf> [Accessed on 03/05/11].

UN Habitat, 'Strategy Paper on Youth in Africa: A Focus on the Most Vulnerable Groups', 2005, pp. 5-37, A paper presented by UN Habitat in conjunction with New Partnership for Africa's Development (NEPAD). Available online at <http://www.gpean.org/aaps/strategypaperenglish.pdf> [Accessed on 26/09/11].

About the Author

Dr. Richard Ayo Adekoya is a pastor, preacher, and scholar of international repute. He is theoretically, pragmatically, and spiritually sound. As a teacher, missionary, counsellor, and theologian, Dr. Adekoya has made a positive impact on a number of lives through his various initiatives, backed by enviable and highly impressive credentials that separate him as a frontrunner and motivator for young people within the church and academia. Dr. Adekoya has been pastoring and lecturing for over two decades in both Nigeria and the United Kingdom. He received a Bachelor of Science degree from the University of Lagos, Nigeria; a Master of Theology degree from Carolina University of Theology, United States of America; a Master's degree in Missional Leadership from University of Wales, United Kingdom; and a Doctor of Ministry degree from Bangor University, Wales, United Kingdom.